THE SUNDAY TIMES

how
i
made
it

40 successful entrepreneurs reveal all

Rachel Bridge

KOGAN
PAGE

Publisher's note
Every possible effort has been made to ensure that the information contained in this book is accurate at the time of going to press, and the publishers and author cannot accept responsibility for any errors or omissions, however caused. No responsibility for loss or damage occasioned to any person acting, or refraining from action, as a result of the material in this publication can be accepted by the editor, the publisher or the author.

First published in Great Britain in 2005 by Kogan Page Limited
Reprinted 2005 (twice)

120 Pentonville Road
London N1 9JN
United Kingdom
www.kogan-page.co.uk

© Rachel Bridge, 2005

ISBN 0 7494 4311 1

British Library Cataloguing-in-Publication Data

A CIP record for this book is available from the British Library.

Typeset by Saxon Graphics Ltd, Derby
Printed and bound in Great Britain by Thanet Press Ltd, Margate

Contents

Praise for *How I Made It*

"Read this book to inspire you when the going gets tough, to reassure you when you've run out of ideas and to give you a kick up the backside when you are feeling sorry for yourself. But whatever you do – read it."
Reading Chronicle

"Thought-provoking and enlightening."
Accounting & Business

"Wage slaves yearning for freedom will be inspired by these relentlessly successful people."
The Times

"Lively, inspiring portraits."
Business Plus

Acknowledgements

I would like to thank all the entrepreneurs for agreeing to be interviewed for this book and for their generosity in sharing their experiences.

I would also like to thank Jon Finch and all those at Kogan Page for helping me turn an idea into reality.

Thank you to *The Sunday Times* for supporting this project, especially Editor John Witherow, Business Editor William Lewis and Managing Editor Richard Caseby. A big thank you also to Kathleen Herron and Rebecca Chambers for all their encouragement.

Finally, thank you to my friends and family, especially my sister Sarah, for all their good advice.

Rachel Bridge
London

The articles in this book originally appeared in the 'How I made it' column in the Business Section of *The Sunday Times* during 2003 and 2004. All have been completely revised and updated for inclusion in this book.

The publisher would like to acknowledge the following photographic copyrights:

4 ©the photo biz; 11 © Martin Beddau @ Cyclop Images; 17 © Paul Chave; 22 © John Deehan; 26 © Chris Close; 39 © Patrick Pope; Author's photo © Lisa Bowerman.

Introduction

There is something incredibly exciting about the idea of becoming an entrepreneur. Just like the dashing hero or plucky heroine in the fairy tale, it's all about starting out with nothing but a desire to succeed, and then using your wit and skill to overcome hurdles and challenges on the way to eventually triumph over disaster and claim your prize.

Unfortunately real life is not always quite that straightforward. Every year thousands of hopeful entrepreneurs in this country decide to take the plunge and start up a business of their own. And every year thousands fail. Regardless of how you measure it, it is a stark fact that well over half of all start-up businesses fail within the first three years.

So what is it that marks the line between success and failure? Why is it that some entrepreneurs race ahead to glory while others fall at the first hurdle?

As the Enterprise Editor of *The Sunday Times* I am privileged to have been able to spend the past few years talking to entrepreneurs about what makes them tick. This book tells some of their stories. Through personal in-depth interviews, 40 successful entrepreneurs explain how they managed to defy the statistics and triumph over the odds to turn their dreams into reality. How they got started. How they found the money they needed, how they decided what to do and how they went about it. How they made it a success. But it also tells how some of them made stupid mistakes, how some had doubts, and how others encountered overwhelming frustrations and difficulties. And how for some there were times when everything went wrong and they sat down and wept because it was just all too hard. If you have ever dreamt of starting up a business of your own, this book is for you.

Some of the people included in this book you will already of heard of. Others you may not – although the chances are you will hear a lot more of them in the future as their success grows. All of them were chosen because they started up their own businesses from scratch and despite everything have survived and thrived. They all have inspiring stories to tell.

There are many theories about what it takes to be a successful entrepreneur, and for someone looking in from the outside most of them sound fairly daunting. There is a widely held perception that you have to start young, preferably while you are still at school. That you have to risk everything – give up your steady job, make sacrifices in your personal life, and put your home and life savings on the line. That you have to have been thinking of brilliant business ideas from birth, and preferably made your first million by the time you are 17.

The good news is that all these are just that – theories. As you will see as you read this book, the majority of successful entrepreneurs do not belong to a special breed of supermen and women blessed with special powers so that everything they touch instantly turns to gold. In reality most entrepreneurs are people just like the rest of us, who forget their door keys, lose vital phone numbers and leave things on trains.

They come in all shapes and sizes. They can be old or young, well educated or not, male or female, naturally confident or painfully shy. They can be the type of person who dreams up a dozen new business ideas a day or the sort who has only ever have had one – which may not even be original. In fact what makes the whole idea of becoming a successful entrepreneur so very exciting is that there are no rules.

Age

Perhaps one of the most reassuring aspects of reading through these interviews is they explode the myth that you have to start young to be a successful entrepreneur. John Mudd was in his mid-fifties by the time he felt brave enough to take the plunge and start up his own snack company. Stephanie Manuel spent decades secretly dreaming of setting up a theatre school for children while she raised a family of her own. She finally got the opportunity to turn her dream into reality at the age of 44.

Professor Colin Gray, Professor of Enterprise Development at the Open University, says: 'Research shows that many successful entrepreneurs do not actually start off straight away. Instead they acquire the skills they need by working for someone else so by the time they set up on their own they are able to draw on many years of working experience. As a result their businesses often go on to survive longer than others.'

Neither do you have to have shown signs of being entre-preneurial in childhood to make a success of it as an adult. Many of the entrepreneurs included in this book did find inventive ways of making money as children – Mark Mills, for example, started selling bags of broken biscuits to his school friends at the age of 6 and by the age of 18 was organ-ising parties in nightclubs. But others were forced by circumstances to curb their creative instincts until they were much older. Rosemary Conley, who went on to create a £13 million business empire of diet books, exercise videos, television shows and a nationwide chain of diet and fitness clubs, was a sickly child who suffered from asthma and, in her own words, was not a very significant child. Mark Wilkinson was an unrecognised dyslexic who spent most of his school days staring out of the window.

Professor Marilyn Davidson, professor of Managerial Psychology at Manchester Business School, says getting the timing right is a far more important element in becoming a success than at what age you start at: 'The stage of life you are at matters much more than your actual age. I think someone can become a successful entrepreneur at any age.'

Inspiration

One of the things that often deters would-be entrepreneurs from taking the plunge is the lack of a good idea. So where do successful ideas come from?

For some people in this book the answer lay in creating something they needed in their own lives. Heather Gilchrist decided to open a children's nursery in Edinburgh because when she tried to find one for her son she discovered that all the good nurseries were already full. Darren Richards set up an Internet dating agency because he was single and wanted to find a girlfriend.

Others decide to turn their hobbies into a business. Rory Byrne had skied every year from the age of four in the same resort in Switzerland, so it was a logical step to start up a company offering skiing holidays there. Trisha Mason bought an old water mill in France for her family to use, but when friends asked for her help in buying properties of their own in France she realised she could use the knowledge she had gained to set up her own business doing that. Some were simply inspired by the belief that they could make a product which was better than anything else out there. Mandy Haberman invented a non-drip drinking cup for toddlers because she realised that there was nothing else on the market which did the job as effectively. Sharon Hilditch invented an anti-ageing machine after working in a cosmetic surgery hospital and deciding that had to be a gentler way of treating skin.

Still others never actually had the idea themselves – they simply adopted a concept they had already seen working successfully somewhere else in the world. Harry Cragoe decided to start selling smoothies in this country after discovering how popular they were in California. Rik Hellewell got the idea for his oven-cleaning business after a friend returned from a holiday in New Zealand and told him about a mobile oven-cleaning business he had seen.

Ros Taylor, a chartered business psychologist who runs her own practice, says: 'You don't have to reinvent the wheel to be a successful entrepreneur. People often find their inspiration from utterly mundane things. The secret is to be able to spot a gap in the market and then be able to fill that gap.'

In fact what is so inspiring is the diversity of areas in which entrepreneurs have been able to flourish. This book includes people who have managed to make fortunes doing everything from selling flowers to repairing computers, from putting on concerts to building gyms.

Professor Gray says: 'Successful entrepreneurship is basically a successful commercial application of an innovation. That could be a new product or a new process, a new way of marketing or a new way of organising people. It could even be something which already exists somewhere else but simply put in a new context. The key is being able to turn it into a commercial success.' He adds: 'A successful entrepreneur can look at something and see an opportunity where you or I would just see an everyday thing. And that to me is really quite magical.'

Finance

One area where many entrepreneurs in this book have had to be particularly inventive is in finding the funds to get their ideas off the ground. With banks nowadays extremely wary of lending money to anyone without a previous track record, most had to approach the problem from another angle.

Daniel Mitchell funded his first company selling office equipment entirely on credit provided by suppliers after he realised he could pay them 30 days later than his customers paid him.

Philip Hughes started his ice-making business with the help of a £5,000 grant from Wandsworth Enterprise Agency. Indeed the secret for many was simply to think creatively. Jane Packer began her flower business in a workroom in a hotel, getting it rent-free in return for providing the hotel with flower arrangements. Penny Streeter launched her recruitment business from a borrowed desk in the corner of a friend's office.

Professor Gray says: 'Successful entrepreneurs are risk takers, but they are controlled risk takers. They are not reckless. And the best way of controlling financial risk is to get others to share the risk with you.'

For Stephanie Manuel, however, getting the money was simply a case of being in the right place at the right time. After years of dreaming of starting up a theatre school for children, by chance she met someone at a party who agreed to put up all the money she needed, in return for a 50 per cent share of the business. It does not get much better than that.

Qualifications

One of the most intriguing aspects of successful entrepreneurs is that many of them left school without any qualifications. Duncan Bannatyne is just one of those interviewed for this book who left school at 15 without an O level to his name. There are a couple of possible reasons for such a link. Without formal qualifications it is not possible to gain entry to the traditional career paths such as accountant, doctor or lawyer, so if people want to become a success they have to find ways of doing it on their own terms. At the same time if you have never had a chance to prove your ability at school, it may make you even more determined to do so later in life.

Professor Gray says that successful entrepreneurs are often highly intelligent people, but they tend to require other types of skills than those that are purely academic. He says: 'Successful entrepreneurs tend to be brighter than other people and they are usually particularly good at people relationship skills. A key part of being an entrepreneur is having the ability to talk to people and communicate with them and persuade them that their idea is a good one. You often find that a lot of successful entrepreneurs are backed by a loyal team.'

Having a university education does not necessarily extinguish the entrepreneurial spirit, however. Indeed for Matt Stevenson, who got a first class degree from Derby, his final dissertation to design an aquarium filter for specialist corals led directly to a business making fish tanks.

Risk

The popular image of the successful entrepreneur is someone who is willing to risk everything to take the plunge and follow a dream. However one comforting aspect for those of a more cautious nature is that contrary to the stereotype, it is not always essential to quit your job, remortgage the house and sell the car in order to take the entrepreneurial route. Gerry Pack secretly kept his full-time job with a holiday company for a full year while getting his hotel booking business off the ground, working on it at evenings and weekends until he felt confident enough that it had a viable future to quit his day job. Maria Kempinska continued in her day job as agent's assistant when she started up her first Jongleurs comedy club and only quit when it was clear that the club was going to be a success.

Chartered business psychologist Ros Taylor says: 'There are those entrepreneurs who have taken big risks but it doesn't have to be that way. You don't necessarily have to jump over the precipice without a parachute. Instead you can plan your venture bit by bit and gradually wean yourself off the company you work for. You don't have to be completely daft.'

Indeed while some entrepreneurs have it all planned out right from the start, others stumbled into entrepreneurship simply by doing what they enjoyed doing, and so never had to make a giant leap into the unknown. Mark Ellingham wrote his first *Rough Guide* travel book because he was not able to find a job after leaving university. It became such a success that it spawned an entire publishing empire. Christopher Wray took up selling antique lamps entirely by chance when as an out-of-work actor he took a stall in Chelsea Antiques Market.

Motivation

So what exactly is it that drives someone to take the entrepreneurial route? The obvious answer is the chance to make a lot of money. But as the stories in this book show, in most cases money is only part of the answer, and sometimes it does not figure at all.

Some people are driven by an overwhelming desire to prove to others that they are capable of achieving something great. Derek Beevor, who now flies to work in a helicopter each day, says he was determined to prove wrong a teacher who told him to leave school because there was no point in his staying on to take O levels. Sarah Doukas, who set up her own modelling agency, says she is motivated by the desire to prove to her father, who had wanted her to follow a profession as a doctor or lawyer, that she could achieve success on her own terms.

Professor Gray says that while most successful entrepreneurs are driven by an innate self-belief and self-confidence, there are a small group of entrepreneurs who are driven primarily by a fear of failure. The outcome is the same, but the causes are very different. He says: 'What drives them is determined by their own experiences. Criticism early in life leads to a fear of failure whereas praise leads to a need for achievement.'

Either way, says Ros Taylor, successful entrepreneurs are usually not primarily motivated by the desire to become rich. She says: 'Money is not the main driver for entrepreneurs. Instead they are motivated by the desire to be in control, to do their own thing and put their stamp on it. Money comes secondary to that. They would obviously rather have money than not, but their motivation is the excitement of seeing what they believe in come to fruition. That is probably why the concept of risking money matters less to an entrepreneur.'

Sibling rivalry can also play an important role. Stephanie Manuel was driven by the desire to prove she was just as good as her two elder brothers, both of whom had achieved great success in their respective professions. Others are simply motivated by the desire to make a difference. Lizzie Vann started up her baby food company in order to improve the quality of children's food because having suffered from asthma and eczema as a child, she believed there was a strong link between nutrition and health. Harry Cragoe started selling smoothies in Britain because he believed passionately that they were good for people and would improve their lives.

Attitude

So what does it take to become a successful entrepreneur? It all comes down to having the right attitude.

The first requirement is to have absolute passion and total belief in what you are trying to achieve. Ask Harry Cragoe to tell you about his smoothies and he will happily talk about them for hours. The same passion for their business applies to everyone else in the book. If you do not believe 100 per cent in what you are doing, you will never be able to persuade anyone else – investors, customers, bank managers, partners or employees – to believe in it either.

Psychologist Ros Taylor says: 'The secret is to tap into what motivates you. You are much more likely to make a success of something if you love what you are doing and have a passion for it. It is that passion which will sustain you through the long dark nights.'

The second is an ability to see every failure as an opportunity, not a disaster. Indeed many of the entrepreneurs in this book did not find success until they had tried several business ventures. When Chris Gorman lost £500,000 setting up a record company which went bust within a year, his first reaction was relief that he had not done it later in life when he might have lost £20 million. His second was to regard the episode as a valuable learning experience because it taught him to stick with businesses he understands.

Professor Marilyn Davidson says: 'If a business fails a true entrepreneur will just pick themselves up and start all over again. They don't dwell on failures; they learn from them and don't let it get them down. But just as important, unlike most other people entrepreneurs will also learn from their successes as well as their mistakes. They will look at things that don't work and analyse why they didn't, but they will also look at things that do work and analyse them too.'

The next requirement is persistence and a refusal to give up. Darren Richards had tried so many disastrous money-making ventures that his friends would tease him about it every time he met them for a drink. But he was determined to prove he could achieve success somehow and so he eventually did. Professor Davidson says: 'Successful entrepreneurs have this hardiness about them which means that they dwell on the positives rather than the negatives. If there is any light at the end of the tunnel then they will follow it.'

Along with persistence, successful entrepreneurs also need endless amounts of optimism.

Ros Taylor says: 'If you ask an entrepreneur how they became so successful, many of them are likely to say they have been really lucky. That answer can be infuriating to other people, especially when it is clear that the entrepreneur has put a lot of hard work into their venture. But they are right in one sense because research shows that if you feel lucky then your chances of being lucky actually increase.' She adds: 'Positive thinkers are much more likely to be successful in everything they undertake because if you feel optimistic you are much more likely to be relaxed – which means you are less likely to be stressed and become ill and have accidents. And so you are likely to live longer. There is a whole pattern of behaviour, which follows from being a lucky and optimistic thinker. They take the view that I can do this, I can solve this, I can make it happen. And so they do.'

A successful entrepreneur also needs to have the ability to spot a potential opportunity, however unlikely, and then make the most of it. Mark Mills made his first million after wondering why no one advertised on the side of post boxes. He was not the first one to spot the opportunity – as the man at the Post Office wearily explained, he was the 50,000th person to have rung them with the idea. But he was the only one of the 50,000 who enrolled on a law degree specifically to see if there was a loophole in the law which would enable him to turn his vision into reality. There was.

Ros Taylor says: 'To be a good entrepreneur you have got to be good at problem solving. And that means being an optimist because by looking for a solution to a problem in your mind you are in effect saying that there has always got to be a way to overcome any difficulties. It is having that constant belief that there will always be a way forward that separates successful entrepreneurs from everyone else.'

With that comes the confidence to change direction when it becomes clear that the path you are pursuing is not leading anywhere. Professor Marilyn Davidson says: 'The secret to success is having the courage to drop an idea when you realise it is not going to work. Successful entrepreneurs are not afraid to start again.'

Conclusion

So the message of this book is this. It is evident from the diversity of experiences detailed here that there is no blueprint to becoming a successful entrepreneur and no right or wrong way of going about it. What really matters is having the right attitude, which means that if you really want it badly enough, you have as much chance as anyone else of defying the statistics and becoming one of the success stories.

Ros Taylor says: 'We are all much more creative than we think. Everyone has it in them to become an entrepreneur. The secret is to adopt a positive attitude and to raise your eyes towards the horizon. It is about being willing to take a few risks, having the courage to break the mould and not just automatically following a set pattern in your life.'

As the entrepreneurs in this book show, all you really need is the determination to make it work, the persistence to keep at it when things go wrong, and the absolute conviction that anything is possible if you really believe in it enough. And the courage to make up your own rules on the way.

I hope this book will inspire you. Good luck.

1

Lizzie Vann
Founder of Organix brands

When Lizzie Vann first hit on the idea of making healthy organic food for babies, she decided to draw up a list of the most nutritional ingredients she could find and then mix them together to create the ultimate superfood. Unfortunately, the three foods at the top of her list were blackberries, lean steak and peanut butter. The experiment was not a great success.

She says: 'I ended up with this horrid, grey, slimy mess that looked like a squashed slug.'

Happily her subsequent attempts to create good food for children worked rather better. A decade on, her company, Organix, sells 10 million jars of baby food a year and Vann has been awarded an MBE for services to children's food.

Brought up in the Midlands, Vann first became interested in nutrition as a child when she suffered badly from asthma and eczema and had to be treated with steroids. She says: 'I felt I needed to understand my illness and, as I studied the way the body's system works, I started to see there were links between food and health.'

She went on to briefly study biology and ecology at Lancaster University, where she also became actively involved in campaigning for social justice. This included volunteering for housing action trusts and helping to set up a wholefood worker co-operative.

Her campaigning took a temporary back seat as she pursued a career as an investment analyst with a firm of actuaries in the City. But after eight years she realised she wanted to get back to the issues she believed in. She says: 'I have always wanted life to feel like it has a coherent pattern to it and made sense instead of putting different aspects of your life in different boxes. But life in the City didn't feel like that. It felt very glamorous and exciting and I felt very important earning lots of money, but it just didn't feel the right thing to be doing as I turned 30.'

'I had always had a very strong belief that society needed to be run in a better way and that ordinary citizens could change things. I started to think there had to be more to life than this.'

Vann decided the best way she could contribute to making the world a better place was to give infants the best possible start in life by creating baby food using organic products and natural ingredients, without additives or chemicals.

She says: 'Babies and children need good food because their bodies are developing and growing and I wanted to make food that would make a difference to their health. I wanted to be a standard setter for the industry.'

Confident that success was just around the corner she quit her job in the City and began experimenting with recipes in her kitchen with the help of a friend.

She says: 'I thought, oh I can do this, it's easy. I decided I needed half a million pounds and thought, I know people in the City, so I'll just go and see them. How naive can you be?'

Unsurprisingly her lack of any experience in setting up a food company did not impress. After being turned down by dozens of venture capitalists and merchant banks she was forced to scale down her ambitions. She started up the company with a more modest £50,000, raised through loans from banks and friends.

Fact file

Date of birth: 23 September 1958

Marital status: long-term partner

Highest level of education achieved: University (did not complete course)

Qualifications: three A levels

Interests: Organic farming and gardening, reading, politics

Personal philosophy: 'Live life in the present. And never forget that information is power. The power of information can change the world.'

She was not even able to persuade a British manufacturer to get involved and ended up having to get the first batch of baby food made in Germany.

She says: 'I visited lots of companies that made baby food but they all said, who are you? Have you ever done this before? What backing have you got? So there was a bit of a credibility gap.'

Her belief in what she was doing started to pay off only when she took a stand at an exhibition for health visitors in Torquay.

She says: 'Baby food had a really bad reputation for being beige and adulterated with maltodextrin and corn flour, so none of the manufacturers would offer its food at exhibitions because people would turn up their noses at it. They gave away things like calculators instead. But we put out bowls of our baby foods for people to taste. They were bright orange and green and purple because they were made with carrots or spinach or blueberries, and people tried them and thought they were great. You could tell what they were by looking at them and tasting them rather than looking at the label.'

Orders from supermarkets quickly followed. Organix now produces around 50 varieties of food for babies and children up to 10, and sales for 2004 will be £16 million.

Vann has meanwhile become a campaigner for better children's food, and in 2003 launched a drive for a children's food bill after drawing up a code of practice for the food industry. She has also set up a Food for Life campaign to improve the quality of school meals which has so far generated a huge response among parents and schools and is contributing to a major shift in the way people view children's nutrition.

Now 46, she says: 'I really believe in the power of people. I believe we can change the world by putting out ideas and raising awareness, by showing different ways of doing things, and by being noisy and loud.'

Vann says her outlook on life has always been driven by a combination of energy, passion and optimism. She says: 'If I have a spare hour then I think I can do 10 things in it. I'm constantly looking for solutions.'

2

Darren Richards
Founder of DatingDirect.com

Love-lorn sceptics seeking proof that Internet dating really can work need look no further than Darren Richards, the creator of Britain's largest dating service, DatingDirect.com. When Richards decided to try out the website he had created, he met the girl of his dreams, Claire, on his second date. That was more than five years ago and they have been together ever since. He says: 'We got on really well, so at the end of the evening I told her I needed to tell her something. She didn't believe who I was until I showed her my business card.'

Bought up in Worcestershire, Richards always dreamt of setting up his own business. He admits: 'I didn't really pay much attention to getting good grades and certificates at school because I was so confident that I would be working for myself I thought I wouldn't need to convince anyone else of my ability.' When he left school at 16, however, he ended up getting a job as a waiter in a hotel restaurant for several years before going to work as a holiday rep in Gran Canaria. He continued to dream about setting up his own business, however, and was always coming up with

potential money-making schemes, such as a loyalty card for high street shops.

He says: 'My mind was always elsewhere, even when I was waiting on tables in the restaurant. I tried so many different things that my friends would say, oh here comes Darren, I wonder what new idea he has today.' He was trying to make a living importing electronic toys from Japan when he hit on the idea of setting up a dating service while idly surfing the Internet one evening at home. Aged 33 and single, having recently come out of a long-term relationship, he suddenly realised that the Internet could be the perfect way of meeting other singletons in his area. But when he searched for an online agency to join, he could only find companies based in America. Even worse, none of the sites seemed to take the idea of meeting a new partner online seriously, encouraging members to use silly nicknames such as Sexy Babe and Hot Pants. He says: 'It was frustrating. I thought I couldn't be the only person who wanted to use the Internet to find a serious date.'

Richards drew up a blueprint of what he thought a British online dating service should be like. Then he spent the next three months researching the market, conducting straw polls with people in the street and asking his friends for their views. Encouraged by their response he bought some software and a couple of website magazines. Then he built a simple site where people could post details of themselves.

He says: 'It was a very basic service and didn't work that well. But it was getting a lot of hits and it proved to me there were a lot of people out there who wanted to use it.' Inspired by the success of his prototype, Richards decided to create a fully-fledged dating website through which members could contact each other directly.

The first few website developers he approached told him it could not be done, but he eventually found someone able and willing to do the job. Richard gave the designer a 20 per cent stake in the company in return for creating a new interactive website, and it was launched in 1999 at a cost of £2,500. Within three months it had 40,000 members.

But Richards still had a big problem. In order to start making money he needed to get people to pay for using his service, and the only way they would do that was if they could pay online by credit card. Barclaycard, however, was

Fact file

Date of birth: 8 May 1966

Marital status: long-term partner

Highest level of education achieved: secondary school

Qualifications: five O levels

Interests: travel, sports cars, taking flying lessons

Personal philosophy: 'You only get one crack at a big opportunity so make sure you recognise it and grab it with both hands.'

not interested in letting him use its facilities. He says: 'It was a nightmare. I knew the company wouldn't survive unless we could take credit-card payments. But we were turned down three times by Barclaycard because they felt that a dating service was a high-risk area in the same category as gambling and pornography.'

Refusing to take no for an answer, Richards drove to Northampton to see the man in charge of applications in person, and gave him a demonstration of the website. The man was so impressed he agreed to grant credit-card facilities on the spot. Barclaycard's decision changed everything. Richards gave up his job importing Japanese toys to concentrate on his Internet dating business full-time, and started charging £15 a month for members wanting to contact potential partners through the site.

He soon discovered that a great number of people were prepared to stump up the money. DatingDirect.com now has 1.5 million active members, of whom around half become paying subscribers. In 2004 the company will have a turnover of more than £10 million, generating a profit of several million pounds. As a result the company, in which Richards has an 80 per cent share, is currently valued at between £25 million and £35 million.

DatingDirect has also chalked up dozens of marriages and babies from people who met via the website. It now also supplies a dating service to other websites including Channel 4 and GMTV.

Now 38, Richards says he still can not quite believe he is now the head of a company worth millions: 'I was beginning to think it was never going to happen. But the moral of the story is, if you think you have a good idea then just keep going for it. You may lose some money and waste some time along the way, but at the end of the day you have only got to find one idea that works.'

3

Maria Kempinska
Founder of Jongleurs

The first time that Maria Kempinska put on a show was at her all-girls convent school during Lent to raise money for charity. It was an unlikely debut into show business but it clearly stood her in good stead. When she sold her chain of Jongleurs comedy clubs a few years ago she received a cheque for £8.5 million.

Brought up on a council estate outside Watford by Polish refugee parents, Kempinska did a lot of voluntary work at the local mental hospital while at school. By the time she left she had set her heart on pursuing a career in psychiatry. But her father refused to allow it, believing she was too young to deal with such a difficult subject, so she decided to train as a teacher instead.

She soon realised she did not want to be part of the school system, however, and started teaching drama in play centres and youth clubs instead.

Kempinska drifted through a series of jobs until, in the early 1980s at the age of 23, she was hired to promote a poet who was performing at the Edinburgh Fringe Festival. It

was the first time she had been to the festival and she loved it. More than that, though, it proved to be just the inspiration she needed.

She says: 'I decided that what London needed was a platform for young new talent like they had in Edinburgh.'

She returned to London full of enthusiasm and started looking around for a possible venue for her club where comedians, poets and musicians could perform. Then she remembered an enormous room above a pub in Battersea, south London, where she used to go roller-skating. After persuading the owners to let her use it on a Friday night, she talked her bank into giving her a £300 overdraft. Then she started looking for unknown, but talented, performers to appear on stage each week.

'I had very little idea about business,' she says. 'But I thought that if the club didn't work and the bank came after me for money then I could sell my bike and pay them back £5 a week.'

She had planned to run the club in partnership with two friends, but when they pulled out she decided to go ahead anyway. She says: 'It was the first time I had done something for myself but I decided I had nothing to lose and so I should just do it.'

She decided to call her club Jongleurs, a medieval term for wandering minstrel.

'I chose a difficult name because my own name is difficult and once people know it, they don't forget it,' says Kempinska. 'So I thought that people wouldn't forget the name Jongleurs that easily.'

It worked. She says: 'The first two Fridays were absolutely packed, and by the fourth week I was getting calls from people asking if they could perform at the club.' There were, however, a few early adjustments to be made. Kempinska's original plan was to have performers of all kinds on stage, but she quickly decided to focus on stand-up comedians after realising there were not enough other types of performers to choose from.

She started running shows on Saturday nights as well, and after six months felt confident enough to give up her day job as an assistant to an actors' agent. Her husband John Davy, joined the business and the two of them ran the

Fact file

Date of birth: 3 May 1953

Marital status: married with two children

Highest level of education achieved: teacher training college

Qualifications: five O levels, teacher certificate in English and drama

Interests: currently studying for an MA in Psychotherapy and Healing

Personal philosophy: 'Walk regularly in your customers' shoes.'

shows in Battersea for eight years. It provided a platform for dozens of comedians who have since become household names, such as Arthur Smith, Paul Merton and Mike Myers.

But Kempinska was wary of relying on talent alone. She says: 'I didn't ever want to rely on a performer to spread the word. The venue itself had to be good enough so people would have a good evening's entertainment – and if they saw somebody who eventually became famous it would be a bonus.'

In 1990 she and Davy formed a partnership with Regent Inns, the company that owned the Battersea venue, splitting all the profits made from the venue equally between them, while Kempinska retained the Jongleurs name.

The partnership went so well that they opened a second Jongleurs in Camden, north London. They also decided to open six further venues across the country, with Regent Inns putting up all the money to create purpose-built venues with a bar, and Kempinska running the comedy club upstairs. She also decided to provide food and a disco after each show.

'When working people go out on a Friday or Saturday night they don't want to go to a room at the top of a scruffy pub which is unkempt and uncared for,' she explains. 'They want to go to a place where they feel that they are getting an evening out and having a good time.'

When Jongleurs had amassed eight venues, the joint venture was put up for sale. It received a couple of offers but in the end Regent Inns itself decided to buy it, giving Kempinska and Davy £8.5 million for their share. Kempinska retains ownership of the Jongleurs name, which she leases to Regent Inns in perpetuity, and has also stayed on as creative director with a contract to provide bookings for all the venues.

Now aged 51, she thinks the reason for her success has been her attention to detail: 'The secret is to know what you are there for – and then to do what you do extremely well.

'It is no good having a venue where the sound is bad and saying you will deal with it next week. You have to deal with it there and then. It is about being the best you can. Do what you want to do, but do it absolutely brilliantly.'

4

Mark Mills
Founder of Cardpoint

If you have ever used a cashpoint machine in a petrol station and been outraged at having to pay £1.50 to withdraw some money, Mark Mills is the man to blame. He got the idea of creating a string of privately owned cash machines after using one in a New York deli. He now has more than 2,100 machines in petrol stations and shops in the UK, which between them generate a turnover of £24 million a year.

Cashpoint machines are not the first time Mills has managed to turn an idea into a money-making venture. Indeed, his CV reads like a whirlwind tour of entrepreneurial enterprise. He started his first business at 18, his second at 20, his third at 22 and his fourth at 25. Cardpoint is his fifth.

He first discovered the desire to make money at the age of six when he starting selling to his friends bags of broken biscuits which his aunt brought home from the factory where she worked. As he grew older, he would borrow his father's cash-and-carry card to buy boxes of crisps at wholesale prices and sell them at school, undercutting prices

charged by the tuck shop. He says: 'I couldn't see the sense in giving something away if people were prepared to pay for it. I kept spotting opportunities and couldn't understand why people didn't fulfil them. Even as a child I could see that the more effort you put in, the more you got out.'

By the time Mills was 18 he was organising parties in nightclubs, hiring a room for £100 and then charging £5 entry fee for up to 300 guests, making a profit of £1,400 in a single night. He left school at 18 just as BT was being privatised, and decided there might be an opportunity to make money by selling new-style payphones, which gave pub owners a better profit margin than the old ones. He did well, but soon decided there was no long-term growth in a business that did not have any recurring revenue.

Mills expanded into mobile phones, but when margins started being squeezed by growing competition he decided there was no future in them, either. So he closed the business and lost £20,000, which took two years to pay off. 'It was a spectacularly terrible judgment,' he admits. 'I got out of mobile phones at the worst time – just before the market took off.'

Mills' next venture was to produce a booklet of dialling codes, but that led to a tussle with BT. Instead he turned his attention to creating a referral system that would put insurance brokers in touch with local tradespeople. It was slow to take off, however, and so in 1997 Mills came up with his best idea yet – advertising on the side of postboxes. He says: 'I phoned the Royal Mail who told me I was the 50,000th person to ring up and suggest it – and the answer was no. But I decided there must be a way round it. I thought perhaps I could produce my own postbox and get the Royal Mail to do the collection from it.'

Unable to get a straight answer out of anyone, Mills enrolled for the first year of a law degree at night school so he could use the law library and figure out if it could be done. He discovered a quirk in the Telecommunications Act that allowed someone to produce a private postbox, provided it had a lock bought from the Royal Mail, which was paid a fee to collect from it. Mills quickly produced a prototype and then asked the big oil companies if they would be interested in having a postbox in their petrol stations. Nearly all said yes. Then he asked Nestlé, the food company, if it would pay for advertising on the side of the boxes. It said yes too.

Fact file

Date of birth: 15 August 1970

Marital status: married with three children

Highest level of education achieved: grammar school

Qualifications: three A levels

Interests: spending time with family, collecting cars

Personal philosophy: 'Give 100 per cent to everything you do – and never give up.'

There was just one problem. Having developed the business, Mills had no money left to put it into practice. He managed to get six postboxes installed before selling the business to the advertising group More O'Ferrall Adshel, staying on as a consultant. The company quickly installed 1,200 boxes around the country, but when it was taken over by another firm the postbox business was put up for sale. It was bought by none other than Royal Mail, which promptly took down all the postboxes and replaced them with their own. Mills, however, did not walk away empty-handed. He had cleverly negotiated a sell-on clause in his contract and received about £1 million from the deal.

Mills was out scouting for new ideas in America when he had the idea of operating his own cash machines. Back home in Britain he discovered that only financial institutions were allowed to become a member of the Link cash-machine network, but undaunted he rang every bank in alphabetical order to find one to sponsor him. Right at the end the Woolwich said yes. His first cash machine started operating in March 2000, and two years later the company floated on the Alternative Investment Market with a valuation of £7 million.

The company, which also runs 3,600 mobile-phone top-up terminals, is now valued at £46 million, giving Mills, who owns 15 per cent, a paper fortune of £6.9 million. It will have a turnover of £28 million for 2004.

The secret of achieving success, he says, is having the confidence to take risks. He has a sign above his desk that says: 'Failure cannot live with persistence.' Now 34, he says: 'You must not be afraid of failure. If you keep going and never give up, then eventually you will turn it round. You just have to keep your nerve.'

5

Penny Streeter
Founder of Ambition 24 Hours

The first time Penny Streeter tried to set up her own recruitment agency it went horribly wrong. Buoyed by her success as a branch manager working for another agency, she borrowed £30,000 to rent luxury offices in Croydon and confidently set up in business with her mother. But it was 1989 and within three months of opening, recession hit and demand for her services dried up, leaving her heavily over-borrowed and spiralling into debt.

She says: 'I took very expensive offices and fitted them out from top to bottom with everything I could possibly get. Fancy photocopiers, big desks, designer chairs – you name it. We tried to work as hard as we could, but I had overextended on cash from day one, so when the business started to go backwards my cash-flow projections went right out of the window. It was just a vicious circle from there on.' She struggled on for two years, but in 1991 had to close the business, losing every penny of the £30,000 she had invested, including £10,000 she had borrowed from her mother.

Streeter says: 'We lost everything. It was terrible. My mother had put every penny she had into the company. It

was basically due to having a lack of business experience. I thought that because I had always been a success I would continue to be a success. But the reality was somewhat different.'

Born in Zimbabwe and brought up in South Africa, Streeter came to England at the age of 16 and went to work as a trainee in an office before becoming a beauty therapist. She soon realised it was not for her, however, and when she walked into a recruitment agency she was offered a job on the spot as a consultant. Streeter flourished and was quickly promoted to branch manager, recruiting her mother to run the other agency owned by the company before deciding to go it alone.

When their business failed in 1991 Streeter briefly returned to South Africa to help her sister run a cabaret restaurant. But when her youngest child caught meningitis she came back to Britain to build a new life here. This time, however, it was in different circumstances. Her marriage had broken down, she was pregnant with her third child and had so little money that she and her children had to live in homeless accommodation provided by the local council.

She says: 'I came back to the UK absolutely penniless. I was at complete rock bottom.'

After months of struggling she decided to get a job in recruitment. But after being interviewed for several positions she realised she wanted to try her hand at starting up her own agency again. 'My mother told me not to be ridiculous. But I knew I could do it. I felt that I had nothing to lose.'

This time round, however, Streeter did things differently. Instead of swish offices and luxury cars, a friend who ran a motor business lent her a small desk in the corner of his office. She explains: 'I had no money and I didn't want to go to the bank because I thought they would laugh me out of the door.' She and her mother worked alternate days so they could share the care of her children, and in the first few years money was so tight that to make ends meet they worked every weekend as DJs at children's parties.

They started off offering secretarial recruitment, but as the business grew they expanded into supplying staff for the financial services sector. Streeter says: 'The difference this time was that I was very cautious about what we were doing. I made sure we built up strong relationships with the people we were recruiting for and listened to exactly what

Fact file

Date of birth: 1 August 1967

Marital status: divorced with four children

Highest level of education achieved: secondary school

Qualifications: none

Interests: water-skiing

Personal philosophy: 'Take life one day at a time because every day is a different day with new challenges.'

they wanted.' She also ran the company in a very different way. She says: 'I learnt not to waste money. The company was run with maximum cost control.'

In 1996 she decided to move onto the high street and changed the name of the company to Ambition. Then one day she was asked to supply care assistants to a nursing home, and suddenly realised the company had stumbled on an untapped market. Streeter explains: 'It is absolutely essential for a nursing home or residential home to have access to good staff, and that they are able to get them immediately, because they are like a hotel that never closes. But we noticed that some nursing homes couldn't fill these positions because they were situated in remote parts of Surrey. It was very noticeable that in this area of the market the service the customer demanded just wasn't being given to them.'

So Streeter decided to start supplying care assistants, often driving them to the nursing homes herself in her car to make sure they were able to get there on time. She also soon realised that nursing homes often needed staff at the last minute at any time of day or night, and so switched to operating her company 24 hours a day. She also began training care assistants to meet the demand, and in 1997 became a licensed nursing agency so her company could supply nurses on demand as well.

The effort has paid off handsomely. Ambition 24 Hours is now a national operation with 19 branches across the country. It employs 200 people and in 2004 will have a turnover of around £65 million.

Streeter, 36, puts her success down to sheer hard work. She says: 'Successful people are the ones who don't switch off from their business. They are the ones who are continually thinking of new ways to move their company forward.'

6

Derek Beevor

Founder of Road Tech Computer Systems

Derek Beevor's photo album would make intriguing viewing. Near the beginning would be a few photographs from his four years in the army when he served with the Parachute Regiment in Northern Ireland. Then, a few pages on, there might be some snaps of him looking like a hippie from the three years he spent travelling round Europe in a Transit van with his girlfriend. They often ran out of money and Beevor was once put in a Greek jail for a month for dancing naked on a restaurant table.

But the most recent photos in the album would show a very different scene – Beevor at the controls of his personal helicopter or standing on the lawn in front of Shenley Hall, the stately home in Hertfordshire which he uses as an office. In the intervening years Beevor, 47, has managed to create from scratch a multi-million pound business selling computer software to the trucking industry.

There was little indication when he was younger that the Beevor story would turn out so well. Born and brought up in Watford, he suffered two early losses: at 11 his father left

the family and at 14 his twin brother died of cancer. He says: 'We went from being a family of four to being just me and my mum. It was quite tough.'

He left school with no qualifications after his teacher asked the class to write down what subjects they wanted to do for O levels – but then tore up the list Beevor had written and told him to leave. He says: 'I was gobsmacked. That afternoon I was gone – mentally scarred for life.'

His involvement with the trucking industry began on a small scale. Back home in Watford after his travels on the Continent and in need of a job, he took the mattress out of his Transit van and started using it to make deliveries for local companies. One of his first assignments was to deliver bread rolls to McDonald's fast food restaurants, which had just started up in the UK. He worked every hour he could and eventually saved enough money to buy another van, and then another, until six years later he had built his own transport company operating 15 trucks.

'Being in the Paras taught me that you just have to go for it and not give up,' he says. 'Once I had one van I wanted two, and when I had two I wanted three. I was probably doing it to get my own back on the teacher who screwed up my bit of paper at school.'

The trucking company was a success, but Beevor realised he was working all week driving trucks and then spending every weekend typing out invoices and sending them to customers. 'I thought there had to be a bloody machine that can do this. But I discovered that all the computers on the market could only do accounts.' He was, however, determined to find a solution, and so asked a small computer company to write him a program that would do exactly what he wanted. When it came up with something he thought he could improve on, he asked one of the company's programmers to come and work for him and rewrite it with him.

The result was Roadrunner, a booking and invoicing system for transport companies that automatically invoices customers at the end of the week. After using it in his own trucking company, Beevor sold a copy of his software to another transport company. When other trucking companies started asking if they could buy it, he suddenly realised he had hit on a winner. Within a few years the software business had become larger than his transport company. So in 1995 he decided to sell the transport operation to concentrate his efforts on growing the software company.

Fact file

Date of birth: 24 June 1955

Marital status: married with two children

Highest level of education achieved: secondary school

Qualifications: none

Interests: flying his helicopter, riding motorbikes

Personal philosophy: 'Nothing is impossible.'

The company now employs 80 people and will have sales of £6 million in 2004. His customers now include the British Army and all the big transport companies in the UK. And Beevor now commutes to work in his Hughes 500 helicopter. He says: 'I'm chuffed to bits about what I have achieved.'

Beevor says however that he has never been driven by the idea of making money. 'Money has got nothing to do with it. I just get a kick out of the business going well. I am really pleased with every sale we make, but I get just as much of a buzz when someone buys something for £99 as I do from a half a million quid deal, because it means that someone is going to use a product that we have made and hopefully they will be pleased with it.'

He thinks that much of his success has been due to realising at an early age that, if he wanted to achieve something in life, it would be entirely up to him to make it happen. He says: 'When I left school I had zero expectations. I just expected to start at the bottom and work my way up. I always knew that I would have to make my own way in life and that nobody was just going to give it to me. I really believe there is nothing you can't do if you put your mind to it and believe in yourself. You just have to listen to your own drummer and not somebody else's.'

7

Rosemary Conley

Inventor of the Hip and Thigh Diet

When 29 overweight women showed up at Thurnby village hall in Leicestershire on a cold winter's evening, Rosemary Conley knew she had found her passion in life. What she did not know was that this passion would eventually turn her into a household name and transform an £8 investment into a £13 million business empire spanning diet books, exercise videos, television shows and a nationwide chain of diet and fitness clubs.

Conley first captured the public's attention in 1988 with the publication of her *Hip and Thigh Diet* book, which has since sold more than 2 million copies. Proclaiming the virtues of eating low-fat food, the diet turned conventional dieting wisdom on its head and Conley into an instant media celebrity. But her seemingly overnight success really began 17 years earlier when her weight ballooned while working in an office as a secretary. After managing to lose two and a half stone, she decided to start a slimming club to help others do the same. Her plan was to go one better than

existing clubs by providing grooming advice and exercise classes as well as diet tips.

After trying out her ideas on neighbours round her kitchen table, she spent £8 getting 30 posters printed and booked the local village hall. She charged £1 to join and 25p to attend each weekly session. She says: 'It was so exciting when people got on the scales each week and I could tell them they had lost as much as seven pounds. They were thrilled. I suddenly realised I was doing something to make people happy. That was so rewarding. I didn't look at it as a big money earner, I just did it because I liked doing it.'

Six months later her classes were so popular that Conley left her secretarial job to concentrate on her slimming club. She opened more and more classes to meet the demand, and eventually sold the business to IPC Magazines 10 years later for £52,000.

It was an unlikely achievement. After leaving school at 15 without qualifications Conley's CV to date had largely consisted of running Tupperware parties and doing any job that would allow her to take along her Pyrenean mountain dog, Sheba. She says: 'I wasn't a very significant child. I suffered from asthma and was quite sickly so the expectations of me were zero. Maybe there was a bit of me that wanted to prove I could actually do something worthwhile.'

After the sale of her slimming clubs to IPC, Conley stayed on with the group to oversee the expansion of the clubs across Britain. But while she appeared to have hit the jackpot, the reality was quite different. She says: 'It was one of the toughest times of my life because I hadn't got the experience or the capability to do such a big job. I felt under a lot of pressure and seriously thought I was going to have a nervous breakdown if I carried on.' She managed to struggle on until IPC decided to disband the clubs a few years later, but the long hours also contributed to the breakdown of her marriage.

In the event it was the pressure of that job that indirectly led to the creation that changed her life. Admitted to hospital with gallstone problems, Conley opted to go on a low-fat diet as an alternative to undergoing surgery because she did not feel she had time to spend months recovering from an operation. The diet not only postponed the need for an operation for many years, but also led to dramatic fat loss.

Fact file

Date of birth: 19 December 1946

Marital status: twice married with one child

Highest level of education achieved: high school

Qualifications: RSA in Exercise to Music

Interests: animals, skiing, interior design, flower arranging, walking, Christianity

Personal philosophy: 'Always have something to look forward to, someone to share it with and always try to make a difference.'

Conley says: 'Right from the start I knew I had hit on something really special. The low-fat diet was an absolute revelation because it worked. I just dropped inches off my hips and thighs.' She got a local radio station to try out her diet on a group of volunteers, and when it worked for them, too, she wrote the *Hip and Thigh Diet* at the age of 41. She was paid an advance of £750. By the time the updated version was published a year later she was paid substantially more – and bought a silver Jaguar XJS with her first royalty cheque.

She says: 'Looking back, I was so fortunate because by the time I hit the big time with the *Hip and Thigh* book I had already had a 17-year apprenticeship in diet and fitness. So I knew what to do.' She has built on the success of that first book to create a diet and fitness empire that so far encompasses 25 books and fitness videos, a *Rosemary Conley* magazine, and a franchise chain of 180 Diet and Fitness Clubs with 80,000 members. She also recently started an online slimming club, www.slimwithrosemary.com.

She says that while it certainly did not feel that way at the time, coming close to a nervous breakdown actually ended up changing the direction of her life for the better. She says: 'It was very tough but I wouldn't be where I am today if I hadn't gone through that painful experience. People say that that there is no such thing as a mistake if you learn from it. And I definitely learnt from that one.'

Now 58, and recently awarded a CBE in the Queen's New Year's Honours List, Conley says: 'The biggest lesson I have learnt along the way is that you can't know everything yourself. If you want to be successful in anything you have to surround yourself with experts who are able to guide you and educate you. It is no different from someone who wants to become an Olympic athlete – they need to have a good trainer and a good manager. Now I only do the things that I alone can do – and let other people do the things that can be done by someone else.'

8

Raymond Gubbay
Founder of Raymond Gubbay Ltd

Concert promoter Raymond Gubbay got his first taste of the performing arts as a child, when his grandmother started taking him to the local theatre on Saturday afternoons. 'Every week there was a different show. We used to sit in the gods for half a crown,' he says. Gubbay also got an early introduction to classical music at home, although he did not appreciate it much at the time. 'My mother was a very good pianist and my dad played the violin, so there was always music in the house,' he says. 'I failed miserably at Piano Grade One, and I tended to think it was all rather boring. But clearly it rubbed off on me a bit.'

Brought up in Golders Green, north London, he left school at 16 to be an articled clerk in his father's accountancy firm. But he soon realised it was not for him. 'It was a complete disaster,' he says. 'I was just not interested in it. After eight months I was six months behind with the correspondence course. I had to leave because I couldn't stand it.'

His father helped him to get a job at Pathé Newsreel, but he did not excel at that either. So his father introduced him

to Victor Hochhauser, a concert promoter who specialised in putting on performances by Russian folk-dance and ballet companies. After an interview that consisted of just three questions – one of which was, can you start on Monday? – Gubbay was given the job of taking folk-dancing companies on concert tours round the country.

After 10 months, however, he decided he had learnt enough to become a concert promoter himself. He had no money apart from £50 his father lent him, but he formed a group of three freelance singers and a pianist, and wrote to dozens of theatres and concert halls across the country trying to get bookings for them.

Fortunately, Gubbay's timing was spot on. The government had recently appointed its first arts minister who was encouraging local authorities to promote the arts and build concert halls. So virtually every town was looking to put on some form of municipal entertainment. Gubbay's first event was a Gilbert and Sullivan evening at the Theatre Royal in Bury St Edmunds, Suffolk. It was a big success, and he was soon putting together other groups of singers and booking them on tours round the country. By the age of 20 he had 150 bookings a year.

There was, however, the occasional mishap. When one of his groups was supposed to be performing in Nottingham the dates got mixed up. He says: 'I had this phone call at seven o'clock in the evening saying where are you? But we were in London. About 300 people had to be given their money back.'

As interest grew, Gubbay formed the London Concert Orchestra from a group of freelance musicians, and started putting on concerts in London's newly opened Festival Hall and Queen Elizabeth Hall. But the real turning point came when the Barbican Concert Hall opened in London in 1982. Gubbay says: 'That was a big milestone. Virtually every performance was sold out because people wanted to go and see the Barbican and to hear the kind of vocal and orchestral concerts I was putting on. It was wonderful.' In the first year of opening Gubbay held 50 concerts there, and by the second year that had risen to 130 dates and he was credited with helping to save the Barbican during its difficult early years.

Gubbay also started putting on exhibitions at the Barbican in collaboration with the organiser of an antiques

Fact file

Date of birth: 2 April 1946

Marital status: divorced with two children

Highest level of education achieved: secondary school

Qualifications: five O levels

Interests and hobbies: living in France (has Paris flat and house in Provence), spending time with grandchildren, French wine, art

Personal philosophy: 'I never forget that there are many more important things in the world than show business.'

fair. By 1988, however, the business climate had become a lot tougher, so he decided to sell his entire company to Emap for several hundred thousand pounds, staying on as managing director.

Emap decided to stage the opera *Turandot* at Wembley, but while it was a success with the critics, the public stayed away. Gubbay says: 'I remember going to the boardroom afterwards and saying, well, there is good news and bad news. The good news is that we have lost under £1 million. The bad news is not by much.' Three years later, he bought his company back from Emap – for £1.

It was an inspired move. He says: 'Buying it back for £1 was the best bargain I ever had. We had had all the disciplines of a publicly quoted company imposed on us, so we were able to run the business in a really efficient way. Turnover went up substantially, and we suddenly found we were making decent profits.' The company quickly created a niche for itself in the market, with shows such as the Classical Spectacular concerts which it puts on twice a year at the Albert Hall.

Gubbay, 58, is thick-skinned about critics who dismiss his concerts as populist and lightweight. 'The critics can be very snooty, but at the end of the day it is about pleasing the public, because they are the ones who buy the tickets,' he says. 'I put on the things that I like and I seem to be in tune with what a section of the public likes, and I think that is important. There is a place for everything. As long as my bank balance is healthy, I don't really mind.'

The company, in which Gubbay still has a majority stake, now puts on 600 performances a year, including concerts, ballet and opera, and in 2004 will have a turnover of £18 million. He says: 'I am motivated by seeing an audience enjoying themselves. It gives me a great buzz. People say to me, you must have had a plan, but I was just enjoying myself and the business just grew. If I'd really wanted to make money I would have done something totally different.'

9

Trisha Mason
Founder of VEF

When Trisha Mason fell in love with a derelict watermill during a holiday in France 15 years ago, she knew instantly that she had to buy it. It was not the most sensible decision to make. The mill had been left to rot for 40 years and had doors hanging off its hinges. And she was single-handedly bringing up two small children in London, having been widowed a few years earlier at the age of 29. She was making a modest living as a freelance management consultant and had little money to spare. But the mill had turrets and a clock tower, and she says: 'I decided that even if the property fell down around my ears we would still have 18 acres of land. We could put a caravan on it and be happy there.'

Mason bought the watermill for £45,000 and spent the next few summers renovating it with the help of friends. When those friends asked her to help them buy properties of their own in France, Mason decided to see if she could make some extra money that way. So she placed an advert in the paper offering her services as a property scout. She says: 'In the early days I used to meet clients at Dover and

then drive them down to the mill in Limousin in my car. They would stay with me and I would cook them five-course meals and then take them out to look at properties for two or three days. Then I would drive them all the way back to England again. It was exhausting.'

But Mason had always relished a challenge. When her children were small, she decided to start a business selling childrenswear and used to stay up all night making clothes. Then, when they began preparing for their O and A levels, she opted to take a psychology degree at the same time so they could all study together round the kitchen table. She admits to being driven by a fear of being bored, saying: 'I have very high energy levels. I love adventure and am always looking for the next challenge. I'm very directed and fast in everything I do. I can't bear people who can't keep up with me.'

Indeed, it was clear to others that she would be a success in business long before she realised it herself. She says that when she was just 19 years old Sir Terence Conran refused to give her a job as his secretary, saying that if he were to employ her she would probably try to take over his job.

Mason says: 'When I got the letter from him turning me down, I rang up and insisted on speaking to him in person to ask why. But it would have been a disaster. He was very astute to recognise it.'

As interest grew in her property consultancy, Mason started taking stands at French property exhibitions in Britain. She quickly realised that the service she was offering in Limousin could be extended to other parts of France. She sold the family home in London and opened three offices, in Charente, Brittany and Normandy, investing the £100,000 equity to set up Vivre En France, now known as VEF.

She says now: 'That was a big jump. I invested all of the equity from the house in the business.' She never doubted, however, that the business would be a success, and thinks her confidence stems from the tragedy of having being widowed at a young age. She says: 'When you lose the most important thing in your life, the loss of anything else isn't terribly important.'

Happily, her timing was perfect and VEF expanded just as the idea of buying a home in France started to capture the

Fact file

Date of birth: 22 April 1945

Marital status: widowed with two children

Highest level of education achieved: university

Qualifications: BSc in psychology from North East London Polytechnic

Interests: growing her own organic vegetables, cultivating her vineyards and olive groves

Personal philosophy: 'Life is about giving other people inspiration to do whatever they want to do well. I like inspiring people to achieve things.'

British public's imagination. 'It was lucky it happened when it did. People's interest in buying in France was just taking off and we were really in at the beginning. Three years ago we didn't even have a London office. Now we have offices in London's Docklands with 35 staff.'

Right from the start Mason opted to do things her way, recruiting native English speakers to run VEF's offices in France as stand-alone businesses, instead of setting up partnerships with local French estate agents as rival companies have done. These guide buyers through the whole purchasing process from translating to legal work for an inclusive fee. She says: 'Most of our clients don't speak French and they need to have someone to hold their hand.'

It's a formula that has worked well. VEF now has 30 offices across France with 20 more in the pipeline. Two years ago the company also started selling brand-new homes in France, Spain and Italy, selling them off-plan to British customers via the company's website and at exhibitions. As a result turnover for 2004 is expected to be around £8 million.

For Mason the adventure is unlikely to end there. Now 59, she lives permanently in the south of France and says: 'Every time I tell people I might let my team take over running the company, they ask what I'm going to start next. I have definitely got one more project in me but next time round I would like to do something which is not necessarily about making money. But I guess I need to earn my place in heaven with this one. I would just really like to feel that I had done something which had made a real difference to people.'

10

John Mudd

Founder of the Real Crisps Company

When John Mudd worked for Bensons Crisps, colleagues would comment on how hard he toiled because he was always the last to leave the office. The truth, however, was rather different. Mudd was staying late because he was secretly working out how to set up a crisp company of his own. He says: 'People were saying gosh, John is keen, he's still here at 9 o'clock in the evening. But really I was writing my business plan.'

Brought up on a council estate in Cardiff, Mudd left school at 15 to work as a porter in a fruit market and then as a delivery driver for a bakery. He discovered he had a flair for salesmanship and so got a job selling sausages and cakes from a van. At 28, he joined Smiths Crisps as a salesman and was encouraged to work his way up the company. 'For the first time I had a boss who recognised some potential in me and gave me the opportunity to develop,' he says. 'I became a van sales supervisor and then a wholesale rep with a car. That was my first taste of going to work in a suit.'

He ended up as area sales manager, but after 15 years he left in 1987 to join the now-defunct Bensons Crisps as marketing manager. Part of his job was to come up with ideas for new crisps, and he decided there might be a gap in the market selling traditional hand-cooked crisps in pubs. The board of the company rejected the idea, but Mudd was so convinced that it could be a winner he decided to do it himself – despite the fact that he was already in his early fifties.

He says: 'It was a bit scary and several people told me it was a brave thing to do at my time of life. But I thought it was a good plan. I also thought that if I left Bensons, there wouldn't be a queue of people waiting to offer me a job so I had better do something for myself.' He wrote a business plan and went to talk to an accountant about how to get funding. Then he conducted some rather unorthodox research by putting Marks & Spencer's crisps in plain paper bags and asking people in pubs what they thought of them. When 80 per cent of them said they liked them, Mudd decided to start The Real Crisps Company making similar crisps. He chose the name Real because it combined his daughters' names, Rebecca and Rachel.

He persuaded a former colleague from Bensons Crisps to join him, and between them they managed to amass funds of £135,000, including Mudd's severance package of £25,000 from Bensons and a £100,000 loan from the bank. Then Mudd leased a factory in Wales and opened for business in 1997 with three employees.

It was a daunting experience. Mudd says: 'The fear started to grip me when I realised that a background as a salesman with some marketing experience did not stand me in good stead for other aspects of being a managing director. It was a hell of a learning curve. For the first two years I worked seven days a week, 15 hours a day.'

He started selling his crisps to pubs and shops in south Wales, but soon realised he had a problem. Mudd explains: 'We were working on inadequate cookers and so the product was too oily. We had a few quality problems and so didn't manage to hold onto all the business we initially got.' He also quickly discovered that the business did not have nearly enough money. Around £80,000 of the original £135,000 raised immediately went on buying and installing second-hand equipment and several months' worth of expensive packaging.

Fact file

Date of birth: 31 July 1944

Marital status: twice married, four children

Highest level of education achieved: secondary modern school

Qualifications: none

Interests: Rugby Union supporter, golf

Personal philosophy: 'You have to be straight with people and your word has got to be your bond.'

He says: 'We could see there were opportunities to expand the business and we had some interest in our crisps from Asda and Tesco. But we were running short of money and it was very difficult. It became pretty obvious that if we didn't get another injection of capital we were going to be in trouble.' So Mudd approached some potential investors, and in 1999 decided to sell 80 per cent of the business to Bar and Restaurant Foods, which occupied the site next door to his factory. In return, Bar and Restaurant Foods agreed to underwrite Real Crisps' bank borrowings.

Mudd says: 'It was a difficult decision, but I am a realist and I knew that without a wedge of money in the business we were never going to be able to grow it. And if we could not grow it, it would die. Bar and Restaurant Foods actually wanted a bigger chunk of the shares than I was happy to give, but I decided that of the potential investors they were the nicest people to deal with.'

Soon after the deal was done, Tesco and Asda started stocking Mudd's crisps. The business is now valued at £7 million and will have sales of £7 million in 2004. Mudd, who became the company's sales and marketing manager, still owns 16 per cent of the company, a stake that is currently worth about £1 million.

Now 59, Mudd admits he was motivated partly by a determination to match the achievements of his brother, who became a university professor. He says: 'Having come from humble origins I thought, well, if one brother can do it, why should he be the only one?' He is extremely proud of what he has achieved. 'When I go into a supermarket and see Real Crisps there, I think that whatever happens in the future, I'm the guy who started it,' he says.

11

Mark Roy

Founder of the Read Group

Mark Roy's first choice of career was short-lived. He performed with the National Youth Theatre as a child, and after taking a degree in creative arts had big plans to become an actor. But when he did not get the first major part he went for, as Romeo in Shakespeare's *Romeo and Juliet*, he promptly decided to forget the whole idea. He says: 'Unfortunately I am not very good at surviving without money. I'm not the sort of guy who can go on for years working as a waiter and attending auditions and being rejected. I decided enough was enough.'

Born and brought up in East Sussex, Roy admits he has always been motivated by the prospect of hard cash. Indeed when his English teacher praised his acting ability and told him he should try to get into the National Youth Theatre, she bet him £5 that he would not be accepted simply to spur him on. Roy says: 'She had obviously latched on to the fact that a financial incentive was the way to my heart.'

After being rejected for the part of Romeo, Roy went straight to the pub to drown his sorrows, and while he was there he spotted a vacancy in a newspaper for a job selling

advertising space for magazines. He got the position and gradually worked his way up through the publishing world, eventually helping to launch several magazines.

He moved on to become marketing director for a travel company. While he was working there he hit on a new approach to marketing that focused on trying to retain existing customers rather than constantly trying to get new ones. He says: 'I turned the concept on its head and started to look at why a company was losing customers. Because losing fewer customers actually costs less than gaining more customers.'

Inspired by his idea, which he dubbed 'negative marketing', Roy decided to invest his life savings of £25,000 to set up his own consultancy advising companies how to put his ideas into practice. Unfortunately, his timing was terrible. It was 1990 and British firms were battling with recession. He says: 'When I phoned up companies to tell them I had this really great idea, they all said, "Bugger off, we don't need anyone else working on strategy because we haven't got the money for it." It was the wrong time, the wrong place and the wrong message.'

But having invested all his savings in the business, Roy could not afford to just walk away. So he took on a contract to supply direct-mail companies with a database of people who had recently moved home. Initially creating the database was simply a way of keeping his consultancy afloat, but then one day Roy realised that he could apply his negative-marketing concept to direct marketing. So he decided to create a database of people who had left their old address, so companies could stop sending them mail.

Roy says: 'Companies were spending millions of pounds a year mailing to people who had not lived at the address they had for them for years. They were just wasting money. I suddenly realised I had a business proposition to put to organisations. I had created a win–win scenario.'

But mail sent to old addresses was just one problem that needed a solution. When his father died in 1999, Roy suddenly realised there was a huge need to create a way for direct-mail companies to stop sending mail to recently deceased people. He says: 'Mailing to somebody who lived at an address 10 years ago is a pain in the neck. But getting mail for someone who has recently died in your family is another kettle of fish altogether. It is distressing

Fact file

Date of birth: 12 June 1961

Marital status: twice married with four children

Highest level of education achieved: university

Qualifications: BA (Hons) in Creative Arts from University of Kent

Interests: golf, wine, cars, gardening

Personal philosophy: 'If you don't ask the question, you don't get.'

and upsetting. Every morning my mother would be inundated with mail addressed to my father, which would remind her he wasn't there any more.'

Roy's solution was to create the Bereavement Register, a database of deceased people which direct-mail companies can use to remove names from their lists. Relatives can contact the register at www.the-bereavement-register.org.uk and get a name deleted from hundreds of mailing lists. So far more than 2.3 million people have registered.

Tragically, six months after the register was launched Roy's wife, Sarah, suddenly died of brain cancer. 'It really drove home what we were trying to achieve with the bereavement register,' he says. 'My seven-year-old would pick up the post from the doormat and say, "Why do they keep writing to mummy? She's dead."'

Three years on, around 1,160 direct-mail companies have signed up to receive the Bereavement Register, which now cleans 56 per cent of all direct mail sent in the UK. The Read Group has 61 employees with operations in Paris, Toronto and Australia. Turnover in 2004 is expected to be £11 million, generating a profit of £1.7 million.

Roy, 43, says his wife's death has made him reassess his priorities. He says: 'Making money is absolutely critical to me and is a fundamental driving force in my life because it gives me choices, but I want to do it in a way that is responsible to other people in my life. I used to work 15 hours a day but now I am home every night to put the kids to bed. I don't want to look back and say, I haven't seen my kids for a decade. It is all about creating a balance in one's life.' He adds: 'It's nice to be able to do well financially, but it's also nice to lie in bed at night thinking I'm doing some good as well. There are so many people who are pissed off doing the job they do and you think, well why are you doing it? Life is not a rehearsal.'

12

Mandy Haberman
Inventor of the Anywayup Cup

Mandy Haberman knew that if she was to have any chance of interesting a big supermarket chain in stocking the non-spill toddler cup she had invented, it had to make a big impression. So she filled one with concentrated blackcurrant juice and sent it by post in a white unlined box to the head buyer at Tesco.

Her tactic worked. Within days Tesco was on the phone. And within weeks Haberman's Anywayup Cup was on supermarket shelves, paving the way for worldwide success and making Haberman wealthy. She says: 'We had sent pictures and flyers and empty samples to Tesco before but buyers receive hundreds of things every day. I realised I needed to give them the wow factor. After all, I had nothing to lose.'

Haberman, 50, had never intended to become an inventor. She was the daughter of an art teacher and a scientist and brought up in Hertfordshire, studying graphic design before becoming a full-time mother of three. But when her daughter Emily was born with a condition that made it difficult for her to suck, Haberman became so frustrated with trying to find a way to feed her baby that she was

determined to find a solution. She says: 'I didn't suddenly wake up one day and think, 'Oh, I'll become an inventor.' It was a necessity thing. The driving force wasn't to create a successful product or to make money. It was because something needed to be done and nobody else was doing anything about it. The energy came from anger. I didn't see why other people should have to go through what I went through trying to feed my daughter.'

She started improvising with bits and pieces she found around the house and would spend hours at the kitchen table trying to create a device which would solve the problem. In the end it took five years of research and endless improvising to come up with a workable model. On the way she had to endure a fair amount of scepticism from friends who wondered why she was devoting so much of her time to such an unlikely project.

But Haberman soon discovered that creating a model which actually worked was just the beginning. She had no money of her own to spend on getting a proper prototype made, and so had to raise the £20,000 she needed by writing to hundreds of organisations asking for help. Then she was unable to find a company interested in licensing her product, which she called the Haberman Feeder. But having come this far she was determined not to give in. So she set up her own firm and marketed her product by mail order to hospitals and parents.

Haberman says that in many ways inventing a solution to help her child was a way of taking back some control over what had happened to their lives. 'When you go through a problem like that you are blown with the wind. You can't change the fact that your baby has a problem, but doing something about it to help other was my way of taking control.' The Haberman Feeder is now used in hospitals throughout the world.

By now the inventing bug had taken hold. Haberman came up with the idea for her second invention while visiting a friend's house and watching a toddler spill juice on the cream carpet. The result was the Anywayup Cup, a toddler-training cup that automatically seals between sips. Creating a valve that was completely leak-proof took many attempts, but finding a company prepared to take it on was even harder, and Haberman made more than 20 presentations

Fact file

Date of birth: 19 October 1954

Marital Status: married with three children

Highest level of education achieved: art school

Qualifications: BA (Hons) in Graphic Design from St Martins School of Art

Interests: walking, the arts, good food and wine

Personal philosophy: 'If you think outside the box, every-thing is possible. Sometimes bad things happen in life but I truly believe that inside every bad thing is a brilliant new opportunity waiting to fly.'

without success. Undaunted, she invested her own money to develop a fully working prototype. The gamble paid off. She discovered a small Welsh company that was willing to work as sales and marketing agents on commission, and within months 60,000 cups were being sold every week.

But then in 1998 disaster struck. One month after Haberman had granted the Welsh company a manufacturing licence to produce the Anywayup Cup, and they had taken on a new factory specially to make it, she discovered that a major brand had launched a similar cup using her technology. She decided to take the competitor to court for infringement of her patent rights. After a court battle lasting 18 months her opponent eventually dropped its appeal, paying costs and substantial damages to Haberman and her team.

It was a nerve-racking process, especially as Haberman realised once the legal process had begun that her family could lose their home if the case went against her. The experience inspired her to start campaigning to promote awareness of intellectual property rights and for a fairer system of enforcement. She is now a member of several advisory committees.

She says: 'The experience was horrendous. I came away from it thinking that nobody should have to go through this. I realised I was in a privileged position to make a noise. One thing I've learnt from litigation is that I am a fighter. To find that I can't just roll over was a revelation.'

Cups using her technology now have annual sales of £10 million. In 2001 Haberman was named Female Inventor of the Year. She has also been recognised by HM Queen Elizabeth as a 'Pioneer to the Life of the Nation'. Haberman says: 'I am proud and somewhat amazed by what I have achieved and I am particularly delighted that the intellectual property system is now changing. I feel that I have made a worthwhile contribution.'

13

Ted Smart

Founder of The Book People

The first job Ted Smart ever had was analysing dog food for
Spillers, the pet-food company. It did not go well. He says:
'On my first day I had to open six cans of competitors' dog
food and smell them. I threw up and resigned on the spot.'

After working his way through another 14 menial jobs in
quick succession he briefly became an air-traffic controller at
Heathrow airport. But when he was called up to do National
Service he decided to head off to Hong Kong instead, where
he got a job as a police inspector. While Smart was there he
started taking photographs of Hong Kong in his spare time,
and decided to publish them in a book. He persuaded a print-
er to let him pay the bill only once the copies had been sold,
because he had no money. He also held an exhibition of his
photographs, which transferred to London where it was
opened by celebrity photographer Lord Snowdon. Smart
says: 'I thought, here we go – it really started my life.'

In 1967, however, Smart was badly injured during the
Cultural Revolution riots and spent six months recovering
in hospital. Later he discovered that his mother had read in
an English newspaper that he had actually died. When he

recovered he returned to Britain, where he tried his hand at publishing another book, this time of photographs of London. Smart says: 'I was always a belligerent idiot and I didn't want to have someone else making the decision whether to publish this book or not. And it gave me the freedom to do it how I wanted.' He stored the printed books in his garage and drove up to London in a van several times a day to try to sell them direct to bookshops.

Smart did well, but after two years he got fed up with driving books around. So in 1969 he set up a publishing company with a friend, producing photographic books. Their big break came in 1981 with the publication of a big, glossy book about the wedding of the Prince of Wales and Lady Diana Spencer, called *Invitation to a Royal Wedding*. It sold more than a million copies worldwide. Smart says: 'It was simply amazing. It changed everything for us. We had no idea it would be that big.'

Between 1969 and 1988 the firm published more than 600 books. As a small company, however, they often found it hard to sell their publications to bookshops. So one afternoon, on a whim, Smart sent an assistant out to Guildford High Street to try selling books to people working in offices. Within a few hours the employee had sold £400 worth of books, more than the company had managed in the previous fortnight.

The idea of selling books this way refused to go away. When Smart parted company with his business partner in 1988 he decided to build a new company from scratch, basing it entirely around the concept of selling books direct to people who would never normally visit a bookshop. He called it The Book People. He quickly pulled together a team of sales representatives and sent them into offices and factories, where they would leave a selection of books for people to look at, and then return the following week to take orders. He says: 'It was controversial at the time because in those days books were only sold though bookshops. But I wanted to go direct to the public.'

Smart also decided to buy outright all the books he needed from publishers instead of returning unsold copies as other booksellers did. This meant that he was able to secure big discounts and so sell his books at much reduced prices. The idea was an instant hit with the public, and within two years The Book People had outgrown Smart's former company.

Fact file

Date of birth: 9 April 1943

Marital status: separated with three children

Highest level of education achieved: boarding school

Qualifications: three A levels

Interests and hobbies: watching Manchester United play, gardening, keeping parrots

Personal philosophy: 'Work hard but make sure you enjoy life too. And always treat people with respect.'

Smart's unique approach did not, however, go down well with other booksellers who felt that The Book People represented unfair competition. Smart is unrepentant. He says: 'I am always being criticised by the industry because I like doing things a different way. But I don't regret a thing. I don't think they understand that I am a great supporter of the industry. Sometimes we just get our wires crossed a bit.'

Not all his decisions were quite so inspired, however. After a few years Smart sold the company to an American firm in return for an annual £600,000 salary and 6 per cent of the gross sales. But after just 12 months he realised he had made a big mistake, and bought the business back for £1.5 million. He admits: 'I couldn't stand being told what to do all the time.'

He also got a horrible personal shock in 1991 when he realised he was supposed to have been on the ill-fated Pan Am flight that blew up over Lockerbie. He only missed it because he had just returned from a trip to America and at the last minute felt too exhausted to fly back so soon.

These days The Book People sells 15 million books a year in Britain. It has more than 2.5 million customers and in 2004 is expected to have a turnover of £68 million. Indeed, it sells so many books that every year its most successful authors, such as celebrity chef Jamie Oliver and Maeve Binchy, come to personally thank the sales team at the company's annual conference.

In 2003 Smart sold a 15 per cent stake in the company to American children's book publisher Scholastic for £15 million, leaving him with a 75 per cent stake valued at £75 million. Now 62, he says: 'Everybody can do whatever they want to do if they want to do it. All you need is belief in your ability. When you start something up, there are times when things go fabulously right and times when they go wrong. You just have to keep your nerve.'

14

Mike Clare
Founder of Dreams

After 12 years of selling furniture for other people, Mike Clare decided it was time he started selling some for himself. It was not the ideal moment – his wife was pregnant with their first child, they were in the process of moving house, and he had a good job working as an area manager for a large chain of furniture stores. Clare had just turned 30, however, and suddenly realised it might be the only chance he had.

He says: 'It was not the best time to start your own business and put everything on the line. But I had been thinking about doing my own thing for years, and as our life was in a phase of change I decided it was a good opportunity to try it. My wife was very supportive and told me I should get it out of my system. She said that if it failed and we were going to have hard times then it was better to do it now rather than later.'

Clare persuaded the bank to lend him £8,000 to add to savings of £4,000. He borrowed another £4,000 on his credit card by claiming it was for a kitchen extension. Then he took a lease on a former motor-spares shop in Uxbridge and

reopened it as the Sofa Bed Centre. It stank of oil but Clare was determined to make it look as good as he could. The night before he opened for business he was still in the shop at midnight on his hands and knees, chipping away at the concrete floor with a chisel to make the doormat fit. On the first day he sold two sofa beds and Clare realised he was on to a winner. He says: 'In the mid-1980s everyone wanted a sofa bed. It was a trendy thing to have and we were on the crest of a wave.'

Brought up in Buckinghamshire, Clare first developed an instinct for making money after his father died when he was 12. He says: 'When my father died I realised that life wasn't going to be as cosy as I had been used to. Suddenly we had to tighten our belts and couldn't go on holiday.' His mother could not afford to keep paying for him to attend a private school so he was transferred to a state school instead, where he was teased because of his posh accent. He says: 'It was a big shock, and I started to understand that I needed to pay a bit more attention to money. So I began doing entrepreneurial things in the evenings and at weekends.'

He started by going out on his bike with a bucket on the back to wash people's cars. By the time he was 16 he was buying batches of used tents from campsites and reselling them through ads in the local paper. He says: 'When people came round to see me I pretended I only had one tent to sell in order to get the best price. If there was a rip in it when they opened it up I would have to make up a story on the spur of the moment about how it happened.'

Within two years of opening his first Sofa Bed Centre, Clare had added three more stores. However, he realised there was a limit to how many more he would be able to open just selling sofa beds, so he decided to sell beds too, and changed the name of his shops to Dreams to reflect the new focus.

Not everyone approved of the new name, however. Clare says: 'My accountant thought it was a stupid name because it didn't say what we did. But I thought it had mileage. It's like the name Virgin – it can adapt to all sort of things and means we can sell anything relating to sleep, such as pyjamas, bed linen and bedside lamps. It is one of our big strengths.' It certainly struck a chord with customers. Within a year of launching Dreams, beds accounted for 80 per cent of the company's total sales.

Fact file

Date of birth: 8 February 1955

Marital status: married with four children

Highest level of education achieved: sixth form college

Qualifications: two A levels

Interests: travel, watching rugby

Personal philosophy: 'Concentrate on planning, people and passion and always live your dreams.'

When Clare decided to take on the company's first ware-house in the early 1990s, however, it became a financial struggle to stay afloat. He says: 'It was very tough and we really had to tighten our belts. I was in the shop seven days a week for six months. But when your house is on the line it really does focus your mind.'

Dreams now has 105 stores across the UK, including seven franchise outlets. For 2004 sales are expected to reach £100 million, generating net profits of £7 million and valu-ing the business, which Clare wholly owns, at about £40 million. In 2002 the company also started manufacturing its own beds in a factory in the Midlands. They are sold to hotels, nursing homes and universities.

Now aged 49, Clare admits he loves his business almost as much as his four children. He says: 'People sometimes ask me why I don't sell the business and play golf instead, but it is like a fifth child to me. I have invested as much time in Dreams as in any of my children and I am very proud of it. It is part of my life and I get a real buzz of enjoyment out of it.'

He thinks success is due to a combination of three things: 'It is partly down to luck, in that maybe our shops were in the right place or we chose a lucky name. It is also due to skill, in that you have to know how to employ the right peo-ple. But the most important element of success is hard work. It is not sexy to say it, but it is about working very hard. Success comes from a bit of luck, a bit of skill and an awful lot of hard work.'

15

Stephanie Manuel
Founder of Stagecoach Theatre Arts

Theatre first became a passion for Stephanie Manuel at the age of 13 when she became involved with a local community pantomime. By the age of 16 she was putting on shows of her own. She says: 'I started off being a performer but I wasn't content to wait from one Christmas to another for the opportunity to be in a show. So I started a youth drama group and wrote plays and hired halls.'

Brought up in Essex and then Surrey, Manuel left school at 16 to go to secretarial college on her father's insistence, and then got a job in an office. But she did not enjoy it and spent every spare moment she could taking part in amateur theatre. 'I spent my days in one boring job after another as a way of making money. But I hated all of them,' she says. 'It was only in the evenings, putting on theatre, that I came alive. At one point I belonged to three amateur theatre groups at the same time.'

At the age of 22 Manuel married a professional actor and then had two children. When she took her daughter to join

the local dancing school she ended up enrolling her seven-year-old son as well, and he turned out to be the one with talent. But when Manuel tried to find a school where her son could learn how to sing and act as well as dance, she discovered there was nothing available. She decided to start a children's theatre school in a disused school building. But when she asked the bank for a loan it turned her down flat because she had no business plan.

So Manuel reluctantly pushed the idea to the back of her mind. When she and her husband got divorced, she focused her energies on bringing up her children, keeping her passion for theatre alive by writing plays and directing productions for amateur drama groups. But by now she was in her mid-thirties and it was getting hard to see where it would all lead.

She says: 'I was desperate to make headway in the world of musical theatre. But I felt I had messed up my chance of having a proper career because I had just been doing odd jobs that didn't interest me.' Her feeling of failure was made even more acute because both her elder brothers were achieving great successes in their fields, with one an international lawyer and the other partner with a prestigious finance house.

When she was 44, however, Manuel met a bank manager called David Sprigg at a party. The chance encounter changed her life. 'He told me his passion was to start a small business,' says Manuel. 'So I said, that's funny because I have a business idea, for a theatre school.' They got talking and decided to start a performing arts school together for children aged between 6 and 16. It would open on Saturdays and after school hours to provide dance, drama and singing classes for children regardless of ability. Sprigg put up the entire initial investment of £8,000 and Manuel gave up her job to run the business full-time while Sprigg stayed on at the bank and helped out on Saturdays.

They opened their first three Stagecoach theatre schools in Surrey in 1988, hiring youth clubs as venues and advertising in the local paper for pupils. The schools went so well that another two quickly followed. Then one day in 1991 a friend of Manuel's asked her if she could open a Stagecoach

Fact file

Date of birth: 3 July 1944

Marital status: divorced with two children

Highest level of education achieved: secretarial college

Qualifications: four O levels, teaching degree in Speech and Drama from London Academy of Music and Dramatic Arts

Interests: horses, spending time with children, reading, going to the theatre

Personal philosophy: 'Persistence pays.'

school of her own. Manuel agreed to make her a joint-venture partner in the school, with her friend running it and Stagecoach taking care of administration, and both sides sharing the profits.

When two more friends asked if they could do the same, Manuel realised the business had real potential. So Sprigg quit the bank to work at Stagecoach full-time. Their faith in the venture paid off. More friends asked if they could open schools, and by 1993 there were 24 Stagecoach schools.

Joint ventures and managed schools required large amounts of administration, so they decided the best solution would be to franchise the business, with each franchisee paying an upfront fee plus 12.5 per cent of turnover. The franchising went so well that in 2001 Manuel and Sprigg floated the company on the Alternative Investment Market, raising almost £3 million to expand the business. As part of the deal they took out £800,000 each for themselves and have kept a combined stake of 31 per cent. The company now has a turnover, including franchise income, of £18 million and is valued on the London Stock Exchange at £9 million.

The success of the company was however almost derailed two years ago by the new Children Act. The Act was introduced to protect children being cared for by nurseries and childminders, but Manuel and Sprigg realised it was so badly worded that it appeared to apply to their schools as well. It would have meant having to recruit twice as many staff as they had – a potential disaster. 'It would have reduced profits so much we would probably have had to close,' she says. In desperation, they lobbied the government for a change in the wording, and after nine months the Act was reworded to exclude Stagecoach and similar organisations.

Stagecoach now has 500 theatre schools worldwide that teach 30,000 children. Former pupils include Jamie Bell, who went on to play *Billy Elliot*, and Zoe Birkett, a recent *Pop Idol* runner-up.

Now aged 60, Manuel says she is amazed at what she has achieved. 'It is overwhelming. It is like a dream. If I am brutally honest, I have always wanted to make something of myself. I have always wanted to have some kind of success and make a difference.'

16

Harry Cragoe
Founder of PJ Smoothies

Harry Cragoe had an early insight into what makes entrepreneurs tick. Most of his parents' friends were self-employed, and at the age of eight he would sit underneath the table when they came round for dinner and listen to their conversations. He says: 'I would hear them talking about their businesses and what they were doing. I'm sure it had an effect on me as I never really considered a life working for someone else.'

He left school at 18 and started working as a commodity broker in the City, but soon quit to set up a company with three friends selling air and water-filter systems. The business took him to Los Angeles where he developed a passion for drinking smoothies, a cold drink made from blended fruit. He says: 'When I left England I was unfit and pasty white, but once I got to Los Angeles I really got into the Californian way of life, going to the gym and running along the beach. And part of that was about putting good stuff inside your body.'

Enthused by his discovery he sold his share of the water-filter company and came back to Britain determined to find

a way of bringing smoothies to a new audience here. He became convinced there was a gap in the market for them after visiting dozens of sandwich bars and discovering that in most of them the only healthy drinks in the chilled cabinet were apple and orange juice.

He asked a friend to help him, and between them they raised £100,000 to invest in the venture. Cragoe says: 'I sold pretty much everything I owned to get the business going, including my flat in Battersea, my car and every investment I had. The only things I had left were my clothes and shoes. I totally believed that smoothies would be a success.'

He quickly discovered, however, that none of the juice manufacturers in Britain agreed. He says: 'People would look at me blankly. They didn't think smoothies would work over here, and they were not remotely interested in helping us make them.' But Cragoe refused to give up on his idea. He went back to America and eventually found a large smoothie maker over there who was prepared to make a batch of 40,000 cases for him and freeze them for shipment to Britain.

Back home he found a designer to create the packaging, and then spent 12 hours a day going from store to store trying to find retailers who might be interested in buying his product. He decided to call his drink Pete and Johnny Smoothies, later shortened to PJ, after two of his friends.

The first order was placed by Cullens supermarket in Fulham, and in October 1994 they took their first delivery. It was not the best time of year to try to sell a chilled drink which customers had never heard of. Cragoe says: 'It was freezing cold outside and they were twice the price of anything else on the shelf. But half of them sold within two hours of being put on the shelves. It was very exciting.'

It was also extremely daunting. He says: 'It was all quite scary because all the time people in the retail trade were telling us that smoothies were just a flash in the pan and that they would be like alcopops, here today and gone tomorrow. I had many sleepless nights.' He was, however, also convinced they were wrong, and to prove it managed to secure orders from supermarket chains Tesco and Waitrose.

British drinks manufacturers were still not interested in getting involved, so Cragoe had to spend two years shipping over frozen smoothies from America – and thawing out each one individually – before he eventually decided to

Fact file

Date of birth: 21 January 1965

Marital status: married with two children

Highest level of education achieved: secondary school

Qualifications: twelve O levels, four A levels

Interests: fishing for trout and salmon, mountain biking, tennis

Personal philosophy: 'Whatever you do, do it at 110 per cent or don't bother, because the results won't please you or anyone else. And be honest in everything you do.'

take the plunge and build a factory of his own in Nottingham. He says: 'It was a major decision to buy our own factory because a factory is a very hungry animal. As you expand you continually need to put more money into growing it and buying more equipment. But it also allows us to have more flexibility in launching new drinks.'

But just as sales started taking off, Cragoe hit an unexpected crisis in his own life. Three years after launching the business and while working seven days a week round the clock, he was seriously injured when he fell off an 80-foot cliff. He had broken his hip, both wrists and a large number of other bones. He was supposed to stay in hospital for six weeks but checked himself out after two week on crutches, which he had specially made for him. He says: 'I had to be back at the office because there was nobody else there to run the business.'

His unwavering determination to succeed has paid off. PJ Smoothies now sells around 350,000 bottles a week in 14 different flavours, and in 2004 Cragoe also launched a lighter smoothie especially for children, called Froooties. As a result turnover for 2004 will be around £12 million.

Cragoe, who took over the running of the business when his partner left to pursue other interests a few years ago, says people should never be put off trying something new: 'I'm not convinced that having experience is that important to becoming a successful entrepreneur. I think that it is about totally and utterly believing in what you are doing and being passionately committed to it.'

For him, setting up his smoothie business has been about more than just making money. He says: 'I am in love with the idea of building a business that improves people's lives. There are millions of people who still are not drinking PJs who I think should be, because they will feel better and will be healthier if they do. It may sound worthy, but that's what drives me.'

17

Rory Byrne
Founder of Powder Byrne

Rory Byrne's love affair with skiing began at the age of four. The youngest of eight children, he was taken on holiday to Grindelwald in Switzerland with his family after his father decided it was time they all learnt the sport he loved. Accommodating the entire family in a hotel was too expensive, however, so Byrne's father bought a caravan and towed it to Grindelwald instead.

Byrne says: 'He persuaded the owner of a caravan site to open in winter so we could park it there. Then my mother and the kids stayed in the caravan while my father stayed in a hotel.' His family returned to Grindelwald every winter to ski, and as Byrne grew up he became good friends with local families. By the time he started university, he was spending all his holidays there, working as a ski guide.

After graduating from university he got a job in the City with a stockbroking firm. But by the age of 23 Byrne realised he had made a mistake. He says: 'I knew I could not wear a suit for the rest of my life and walk in and out of office buildings. And I didn't like being part of a hierarchy. It was like being back at school.' He decided that he wanted

to work for himself, and as the only thing he could do well was ski, he started a holiday ski business.

Byrne rented three chalets in Grindelwald for the 1985–86 winter season, produced a brochure with the help of the stockbroker's production department, and then left his job. He raised £5,000 by selling his car and borrowed £10,000 from his mother. Then he called everyone he knew to see if they wanted to book a skiing holiday with his company. He called the company Powder Byrne as he wanted to teach clients how to ski off-piste, known as powder skiing.

Within a few months he had filled all the 178 nights he had reserved in the chalets. Byrne came back to England the following spring determined to find a way of turning his success into a fully-fledged business. He was wondering how to go about it when a friend who worked in the City told him about a fund being launched by the businessman Lord Harris to invest £1 million in 10 entrepreneurs. Byrne got in touch and was taken on.

The fund took an option to acquire 25 per cent of Byrne's company for £7,500. More importantly, it led to lots of publicity for his skiing holiday business and provided two experienced businessmen to sit on the board. Byrne says: 'They were fantastic. One was a financial guru and the other a really good marketer. We got great advice.'

The company grew rapidly and was soon renting 10 chalets in Grindelwald for the season. But in 1989 Byrne made the bold decision to stop using chalets and switch to five-star hotels instead, installing his own staff at each hotel to look after his clients. 'It was the biggest decision I ever made but it was also the best,' he says. 'People were demanding better quality and by using hotels we could offer luxury accommodation.' He realised that there might also be a demand for teaching children how to ski, so he started up a kids' club which now teaches 1,000 children a year.

In the 1990s, however, things got tough. Byrne says: 'Powder skiing really went out of fashion. Some years the snow was really poor, all the talk was of global warming, and people were saying that skiing would be finished. Even I thought, what is going to happen if skiing stops?' By 1999, however, Byrne faced the opposite problem. So much snow fell that the road to Grindelwald was closed and holiday-makers were stranded in the resort.

Fact file

Date of birth: 1 July 1961

Marital status: divorced with four children

Highest level of education achieved: university

Qualifications: BSc (Hons) in Mathematics from London University

Interests: skiing, sports cars, boats, rugby and wine

Personal philosophy: 'Why be ordinary when you can be extraordinary?'

Fortunately, Byrne had a big advantage. He managed to get in touch with some local men he skied with as a child and through them rented two Puma helicopters. Within hours he had flown out all 140 of his clients. He says: 'Some people were trapped in the resort for 10 days but I got all my clients out and they all made their flights home. It was like a military operation. The Pumas lifted the clients out with their luggage slung underneath in nets.' Byrne footed the bill for the operation which came to £20,000.

Byrne thinks much of the secret of his success has been due to his eye for detail. 'I am always looking at ways of doing things better,' he says. 'I have a phenomenal eye for detail which in the office can be positively annoying. Visually I am a perfectionist, and I will pick up on the tiniest thing that isn't important to anyone else but me. When I see something wrong I want to put it right.'

Powder Byrne now offers skiing holidays at nine resorts in Switzerland and France and handles up to 7,000 customers each season, 85 per cent of whom are repeat clients or have been recommended by friends. The firm also operates a summer season in nine resorts around the Mediterranean. Its annual sales for 2004 are expected to be £10 million.

Aged 43, Byrne now lives in Grindelwald full time with his four children and still owns 100 per cent of the business. He still does not think of himself as the owner, however, saying: 'I have never felt that Powder Byrne was mine. I don't associate the name with my surname. From the first day I started my own company the only way I managed to sleep at night was to believe that I was working for somebody else and that the company just happened to be called Powder Byrne. I never considered myself to be the owner of the company because otherwise I wouldn't be able to switch off from it and shut the door of the office and walk away. And you have to be able to do that.'

18

Jane Packer
Founder of Jane Packer Flowers

When Jane Packer got a call early one Monday morning asking if she could drop everything to meet someone to talk about wedding flowers, she almost said no because she had been working all weekend and was exhausted. However, when the caller insisted, she relented – and went round to discover that the bride-to-be was none other than the Duchess of York.

It was the first time a tiny shop had been chosen over a long-established firm to provide the flowers for a royal wedding, and suddenly Packer was front-page news. She says: 'I was coming back from the market one morning when they announced on the radio that a 26-year-old florist had been chosen. By the time I got back to the shop there were six journalists waiting outside.'

Packer, now 45, first became interested in flowers when she got a Saturday job in a traditional florist's shop near where she lived in Grays, Essex, while still at school. She says: 'It started off as a way to earn pocket money, but as soon as I started working there, I got hooked. Nobody real-

ly understood why because flower arranging was the kind of thing that old ladies did on a Thursday night.'

After leaving school at the age of 17 she started working in the shop full-time, but it was not until she started a floristry course in London that she discovered how creative flowers could be. She says: 'The girls who worked in the London shops would come in with these fabulous bunches of flowers and I would just have a little bunch of chrysanthemums that I'd carried up on the train. It opened up a whole new world for me. In the shop where I worked, people only bought flowers for weddings and funerals.'

She moved to London herself and got a job as a florist in a hotel. When she decided to move on after two years at the age of 21, the manager told her that if she ever decided to start up her own floristry business, she should come and see him. Three months later she was back, having realised that his offer of help was too good to walk away from. The manager gave her a rent-free workroom in exchange for doing the hotel's flowers, and armed with a £500 overdraft, Packer was in business. She decided that a good place to start getting orders might be the gentlemen's clubs on Pall Mall. But she did not have enough money to print brochures so she decided to simply send them a bouquet instead – and quickly discovered that it was a much more effective way of getting her flowers noticed and getting business.

After a year her flowers were selling so well that Packer moved into her own premises in a former café in the West End, but it was harder work than she had imagined. She says: 'I was very naive. I quickly found that the only way I could afford to pay the rent was by working seven days a week, going to market at 5 am and often working through the night. For the first four years I hardly stepped foot outside the door.' Her mother would travel up from Essex one day a week to help with her accounts.

Having her own place also gave Packer a chance to develop her own style. She says: 'I banned carnations and chrysanthemums from the shop and bought all the country flowers I could find. I used to buy sunflowers from a farmer and would go out to meadows at the weekend and pick wild flowers like stock and cow parsley. I have always thought that one beautiful flower in the right vase says as much as a hundred flowers.'

Her individual style was quickly noticed. Magazine stylists started coming into the shop in search of inspiration

Fact file

Date of birth: 22 September 1959

Marital status: married with two children

Highest level of education achieved: secondary school

Qualifications: five CSEs

Interests/hobbies: cooking, reading, theatre and film

Personal philosophy: 'Tomorrow is another day. I am forever optimistic, nothing gets me down for too long.'

and soon she was asked to write a book. Its success prompt-ed so many requests from people to learn about her meth-ods that in 1990 Packer decided the simplest solution would be to open her own floristry school. She and her husband-to-be sold the flat they were living in and bought an old house with a basement which they converted into class-rooms. They lived in squalor in the rooms upstairs until they could afford to renovate the rest of the house. It was a sound move. The school was such a success that within weeks of opening she was approached by a company who wanted to open a Jane Packer school in Japan. Another fol-lowed in Korea.

Ten years ago, however, the company was thrown into crisis after two big clients went into liquidation owing a lot of money. Packer says: 'I didn't know if I could survive this. The bank sent surveyors round to value our house and I was so angry at their callousness. What was so infuriating was that it was through something that was no fault of our own.' Happily, the company pulled through and now has nine retail outlets in Japan, Korea, New York and the UK, where it supplies flowers for Gordon Ramsay's restaurants and fashion designer John Galliano. Turnover for 2004 is expected to be £7 million.

Packer, now 45, thinks her success has a lot to do with her positive outlook on life. She says: 'I'm always optimistic. I never stop to think whether something is achievable or not, I just always think, oh I can do that, it will turn out fine. The only problem is that I can get halfway and then discover I have bitten off more than I can chew. I remember trying to make strudel pastry once – I ended up with it stretched all the way around the kitchen.'

19

Chris Gorman
Founder of DX Communications

Chris Gorman showed his first signs of entrepreneurial flair at the age of 13. He did a paper round each day and persuaded the shop owner to let him organise delivery of all the newspapers because he thought he could do it better. He says: 'It cost the owner £50 a week to run the paper round, so I told him I would still do it for the same money but keep any profit for myself. I reorganised some of the rounds and was able to get the whole thing done for £40. So I went from making £2 a week doing a round to making £10 a week managing it.'

Brought up in a poor area of Hartlepool, Gorman left school at 16 to become a management trainee with a local supermarket. His ambition was to become manager of the store by the time he was 30 and earn £30,000 a year. Then one day he read Dale Carnegie's classic book *How to Win Friends and Influence People*. It changed his life. He says: 'Everything in the book rang so true, the fact that we have this amazing opportunity in life if only we grasp it. I started to wonder whether I really wanted to spend the next 13

years becoming a store manager or whether I was going to do something different with my life.'

He was sufficiently inspired to quit his supermarket job and became a self-employed salesperson selling LED display screens to businesses around Newcastle. He moved on to selling mobile phones and answering machines, and by the time he was 20 he was earning £35,000 a year.

Gorman was convinced that mobile phones had huge potential, so he moved to London where he got a job selling them to large corporate clients. He was extremely successful at it but when his wife became pregnant they decided to move to Scotland, and things took a turn for the worse financially. It was 1990 and the housing market had just crashed, wiping £30,000 off the value of the house Gorman had bought in Wimbledon. He had to take out a personal loan at 26 per cent interest to pay back the mortgage company. Then when he got a job selling mobile phones in Scotland he faced strong initial resistance from customers.

Gorman says: 'At my first meeting the guy said, "I really enjoyed your pitch, but I wouldn't buy anything off an Englishman." I went home that night almost in despair.' But he refused to give up and started spending three nights a week in the local library finding out everything he could about potential customers. His research paid off. Within 18 months had become the best salesperson in the company and earned enough to pay off all his debts and put down a deposit on a house.

Having gone as far as he could within the company, however, Gorman decided it was time to do something for himself. So he left his job and invested £25,000 to become a founder shareholder in DX Communications, one of the first companies in the UK to sell mobile phones through retail shops. It was an inspired idea. Between 1995 and 1999 the company opened 140 stores and grew from £100,000 turnover to £70 million. Just before Gorman turned 30 the company sold a 25 per cent stake to BT Cellnet for £4 million, of which £1 million went straight to Gorman. He says: 'It was a life-changing moment. I ran into the house, saying, "We made it, we made it."' He received a further £6 million when the rest of the company was sold to BT Cellnet for £42 million.

His next attempt at making money was not so successful, however. He invested £500,000 in setting up a recording stu-

Fact file

Date of birth: 25 December 1966

Marital status: married with four children

Highest level of education achieved: secondary school

Qualifications: five O levels

Interests: travelling, playing and writing music, films and charity work

Personal philosophy: 'Good things come to those that wait, but only the things left by those that hustle.'

dio and record label, but within a year had to close it down, losing his entire investment. He is philosophical about the loss, saying: 'It was a great learning experience for me to feel the pain of failure because it taught me that I should stick with the things I know and understand. It was better it happened then than when I had £20 million to lose.'

Undaunted, he decided to turn his attention instead to the Internet, and in 1999 invested £200,000 to start up an Internet consultancy called Reality Group. On this occasion his timing was spot on. Within seven months he had 90 people working for him and an order book of £8 million. After just 15 months he sold the business to GUS for £35 million, reaping a personal profit of £14 million.

Gorman has now turned his attention to breathing new life into existing businesses. In 2002 he joined forces with the Scottish entrepreneur Tom Hunter to take a majority stake in the ailing retail chain The Gadget Shop. A year later the pair also bought the Birthdays group, a national card and gift retailer, with the aim of turning both round with Gorman at the helm. The Gadget Shop is now expected to achieve a turnover of £60 million in 2004 while Birthdays is on target to have a turnover of £160 million.

Gorman, now aged 38, says the secret to being successful is all about seizing opportunities. He also believes that experiencing failure is an essential part of becoming a successful entrepreneur. He says: 'One of the things I love about America is that people accept failure as a natural part of entrepreneurialism. Unfortunately, in the UK, if you fail at something, all too often nobody wants to know you again. But failure can be one of the best lessons. Fear of failure stops people doing great things but learning from failure helps you achieve even greater things.'

20

Mark Ellingham
Founder of Rough Guides

Mark Ellingham had always dreamt of becoming a journalist, but when he graduated from university with a degree in English he could not find a job. So he went on holiday to Greece for a couple of months instead. While he was there Ellingham realised there might be a gap in the market for a guidebook that combined practical advice with a real insight into the country's culture. He wrote a couple of chapters and when he returned home managed to find a publisher who agreed to pay him an advance of £900 to finish it.

Neither he nor his publisher was prepared however for the scale of the book's success. Within weeks of publication, the *Rough Guide to Greece* had to be reprinted twice. Ellingham, who was brought up outside Salisbury by his mother, a social worker, says: 'There hadn't really been a new guidebook series of any note since the 1950s, so in retrospect it was a golden time to write it.'

The publisher quickly agreed to a series of Rough Guides on other destinations. So Ellingham wrote the guides to Spain and Portugal himself and commissioned friends to

write others, editing them in a makeshift office he set up in his housing association flat in Camberwell, south London. Not everyone was enamoured with the Rough Guide concept, however. Ellingham says: 'The first time the publisher tried to sell it to America it got a telex back saying that the name was off-putting. I think if I had planned it, I wouldn't have come up with a name that was quite so daft.' However the title could have been a lot worse. While he was at university Ellingham started up a student magazine called *April Makes Me Vomit*.

Ellingham was busy editing the fifteenth Rough Guide book when the publisher was unexpectedly taken over by another company. The new owners promptly decided that the Rough Guide imprint did not fit in with its plans and put it up for sale. Fortunately Ellingham had inserted a clause in his contract stating that the Rough Guide imprint could only be sold with his permission. So he and a couple of friends, John Fisher and Martin Dunford, who had been helping him write and edit the books, decided to buy it themselves. He says: 'I wanted to have a say in what happened to us. In the end there was only one bidder that I approved of. And that was me.'

Ellingham was 26. He says: 'It was a nervy time. I remember the guy who was negotiating with me banging the desk and swearing at me and saying, "I'll give you £100,000, you just have to sign this bloody piece of paper." It was quite tempting because it was more money than I had ever imagined in my life. But I liked the idea of being independent and the group of us holding our destiny in our own hands. Overnight we moved from being writers and editors to being entrepreneurs.'

Ellingham persuaded a distributor to lend them £200,000 to buy the stock of Rough Guide books that had already been printed. And when the distributor went into receivership a few years later he asked the publisher Penguin to do the same, this time lending them £400,000. He says: 'I just winged it really. If you don't know how deals are supposed to work then you can just suggest exactly how you want them to work.' It was a sound move. Penguin started selling Rough Guides overseas and within three years sales had doubled. The series also received huge publicity, with a Rough Guides series shown on television, which ran for six

Fact file

Date of birth: 8 April 1959

Marital status: married with one child

Highest level of education achieved: university

Qualifications: BA in English from Bristol University

Interests: world music – he is a director and contributing editor of *Songlines*, the world music magazine; watching Manchester United play

Personal philosophy: 'Invent the rules.'

years. The guides now cover 200 destinations and have sold more than 20 million copies.

Ellingham also decided to expand into non-travel subjects. He struck gold with the *Rough Guide to the Internet*, which sold 4.5 million books, making it the company's most successful ever title.

The hard work paid off. In 1998 Ellingham and his partners sold 51 per cent of the company to Penguin for £5 million, then last year they sold the remaining 49 per cent to them for another £5 million. Under a share equity scheme 10 per cent of the sale was distributed to 100 staff and authors.

Ellingham has stayed on at Penguin as Rough Guide publisher in an arrangement which allows him to work three days a week – and not at all during school holidays – so he can spend more time with his wife and young son. He has also started another publishing company, Sort Of Books, with his wife, Natania Jansz. Their original aim was simply to publish a book written by a friend. Ellingham explains: 'A good friend of ours was living on a peasant farm in southern Spain and whenever anyone went out to see him they would end up talking about how he could make it work financially. There was no hope of making much money from the farm itself. But it was the most beautiful place and he had a string of funny stories about life there so we helped him turn his experiences into a book. I thought if we published it ourselves we could probably sell 20,000 copies.'

The friend was Chris Stewart, the book was *Driving over Lemons*, and it became a best-seller, selling more than 500,000 copies. Sort Of have now published 10 books.

Ellingham, 45, says however that he is not remotely driven by the idea of making money. He says: 'I just like to produce things and to make ideas happen.' He thinks much of his success comes from being single-minded. He says: 'I can see an idea and run with it and not be afraid to try it and put money into it. If you believe you can do something better or different, then you shouldn't be intimidated. You have to just single-mindedly plough your own furrow.'

21

Sarah Doukas
Founder of Storm

Sarah Doukas was waiting to catch a plane at JFK airport when she noticed a waif-like 14-year-old girl in the departure lounge. Doukas gave her a business card and told her to call if she would like to become a model. The girl's name was Kate Moss. She joined Doukas's agency the next day and is now one of the most successful models in the world.

Doukas has always done things her own way. Sent away to boarding school at the age of seven, she quickly learnt to be independent and self-reliant. Her parents had hoped she would go into a profession, but Doukas flunked her exams and moved to London to become a model. She says: 'I was put under a lot of pressure from my parents to be academic. As far as my father was concerned, unless you followed medicine or law or a conservative profession, you weren't going to have a reasonable life. But I thought, to hell with it, I'll do whatever I want. I completed one A level and walked out of the rest. My father was furious. He didn't speak to me for two years.'

In between modelling assignments, Doukas started selling antiques from a stall in Chelsea and embarked on a

series of adventures. She went to live in Paris for a couple of years to sell antiques in flea markets and then returned to London to manage a punk band. She says: 'A friend in Paris wanted to sign the band to his record company and had nobody to look after them in Britain so I started managing them. I did everything from driving the van to loading the equipment to setting up their gigs. I didn't get any sleep but it was a lot of fun.'

While managing the band, Doukas met and married an American singer. They went to live in San Francisco, where she set up a children's clothing company. When they returned to Britain four years later in 1982 she got a job as a trainee booking agent in a modelling agency. She says: 'I had always thought it might be quite fun to do. I was delighted not to be modelling any more. I never enjoyed being in front of the camera, I was always panic-stricken.'

After seven years there, she realised she wanted to start her own agency even though it would mean becoming a rival to the company she worked for. She says: 'I knew my boss wouldn't like it but I had this burning ambition to have my own company. I felt bad about it but I was getting frustrated because there wasn't anywhere else for me to go within the company. And I knew I couldn't stay there forever with someone in a more senior position to me.'

However, she deliberately took no action to set up her agency until she had actually left her old job. 'It was a mad thing to do,' she says, 'but I couldn't go to sleep at night or look at somebody at work and think I was organising something behind their back.' Once she had left she asked some accountants to help her draw up a business plan. After much effort she found a backer who would lend her some money. However, just before the deal was finalised, the brother of an old school friend called to say he had heard about her plans and would like to get involved. It was Sir Richard Branson. It was not a situation most other entrepreneurs are likely to find themselves in. Doukas says: 'Thank you, father, for sending me to an expensive school. I shared a dorm with Richard's sister while I was doing A level retakes. It is all about who you know in this life.'

Despite having no money of her own to invest, Doukas was determined to retain at least 50 per cent of her company, so Branson agreed that his private company would

Fact file

Date of birth: 21 December 1955

Marital status: married with two children

Highest level of education achieved: boarding school

Qualifications: seven O levels, one A level

Interests: art, music, horse-riding, farming

Personal philosophy: 'Anything is achievable. Be positive, be enthusiastic, and project confidence. Make every day a good day.'

take the other half. In return he gave Doukas a £250,000 interest-free loan for three years and bought a house in Kensington for her to use as offices.

Her modelling agency, Storm, quickly became known for taking on only the best models. Doukas says: 'We used to turn people down who were actually quite good because I wanted to create a very elitist agency and work only with the high-end magazines. I always think you have to strive for the top.'

Storm also became known for finding models in the most unlikely places – and for taking a chance on unconventional talent. Doukas discovered Liberty Ross shopping on London's Oxford Street, and signed up Sophie Dahl even though she was much larger than conventional models. Business went so well that in 1997 Doukas opened a second agency in Cape Town, South Africa. The following year she also started up an actors' agency in London.

Now 49, Doukas has turned Storm into something of a family affair. Her brother Simon works for the company and her eldest daughter Noelle is a booking agent. The agency has a turnover of £8 million and employs 29 people. She says: 'There has been a lot of luck involved. I was lucky when I started this agency that there was no other agency starting at the same time and the economy was good. And then I was lucky that when we went into recession I had low overheads so we could spend money while other people were tightening their belts.'

Doukas says she has been driven by the desire to prove to her father that she could achieve success on her own terms. 'I am not interested in money. It is nice to have a nice car but it is not my prime motivation. Instead, I have a desire to prove myself. I think I am terrified of failure. Also, I love what I do. It is easy to come to work and do long hours if you enjoy it.'

22

Tim Roupell

Founder of Daily Bread

Attached to Tim Roupell's computer is a scrap of paper that says: 'To avoid seasickness look to the horizon.' He has read it many times since quitting his job as a City commodities trader to start his own business making sandwiches. He says: 'The idea is that instead of worrying about unimportant things you should look at where you are going and not let the small stuff get in the way.'

Born in Wimbledon, Roupell spent his childhood divided between boarding school and foreign postings in Germany, Aden in the Middle East and Hong Kong where his father was serving with the British Army. He left school at 18 and got a job in the City, largely because his older brother already worked there and a position came up in the same firm. Roupell admits: 'It was a real cop-out. I wanted to do something different but there I was wearing a suit and going into the City every day. The money was a big lure. I was completely mercenary and desperate to be independent. Then very quickly I had a mortgage and got used to skiing holidays and found myself staying there.'

But after working as a trader for 10 years he realised he hated his job and really wanted to work for himself. 'I started off enjoying it, but it became soul-destroying. I couldn't bear it. The trouble was I never really cared what the price of sugar or coffee was. I got to the point where I had to do something with my life.'

Having entered the City straight from school, however, he had no experience of doing anything else. He says: 'That limited my options quite a lot. But it was very hard to buy a good sandwich near where I worked in Victoria so I thought that if I could make good-quality sandwiches and deliver them to offices there would be a market.' In the end the decision to take the plunge was made for him when he was asked to leave his job. He invested £800 in a meat-slicing machine and a couple of baskets, and begged a friend who owned a delicatessen to let him use his basement.

He says: 'I literally got up at 4.30 am the next morning and started making sandwiches, and then went round offices flogging them. It was a pretty humbling thing to do. The traders I used to work with thought I was mad.' But on the first day he sold 35 sandwiches and Daily Bread was born.

As sales grew, Roupell recruited people to help him and also started supplying sandwich platters. But it was hard work. 'It was a logistical nightmare trying to get students or out-of-work actors to do basket rounds every day,' he says. 'Sometimes they didn't turn up or they'd have a bad day and sell only half the sandwiches.' After a year, Roupell had taken on five full-time staff and was able to move Daily Bread into its own premises. But in 1996, 10 years after he began the business, crisis struck. Daily Bread lost two big clients, sales slumped and for the first time the business started losing money.

In a desperate attempt to revive sales Roupell decided to open a small outlet in Brixton. It was a big mistake. He says: 'It was such a disaster that I pulled the plug after a month and a half. We almost couldn't give the sandwiches away. And it was at a time when we could least afford to take a punt like that.' It was a tough test of his philosophy of keeping his eye on the horizon. He admits: 'I got incredibly close to throwing in the towel. It would have been a lot of hard work to get nowhere and it was a pretty galling thought. I was 40 years old with three children and I knew I

Fact file

Date of birth: 6 January 1955

Marital status: married with three children

Highest level of education achieved: boarding school

Qualifications: seven O levels, one A level

Interests: playing tennis, skiing, playing the guitar, blues and rock music

Philosophy: 'What goes around comes around. Treat as you are treated.'

never wanted to work for other people again, but I began to realise I might have to. It was not a good place to be.'

He was saved at the last minute by a large order from a contract caterer. Roupell says: 'That was our turning point. We started taking a regular order and then we realised that the way forward was to sell sandwiches wholesale. The margin was much lower, but dropping off 300 sandwiches was so much easier than delivering batches of 20 sandwiches here and 15 there.'

When that order led to others, Roupell took the bold decision to ditch the basket rounds and the platters altogether and focus entirely on wholesale deliveries. He says: 'It was a big step. At the time platters accounted for nearly half our sales so it was quite a punchy thing to do. But I realised that if we offered the best quality and service, then people would use us. And that is what has driven us ever since.'

It worked. Daily Bread now sells 40,000 sandwiches a day and was recently awarded a royal warrant to supply sandwiches to the Queen. Total sales in 2004 are likely to be about £10 million. Roupell is in no doubt about the secret to his success: 'They say that fear and greed are the two main drivers. Well, I am totally driven by fear. Nobody likes to fail and sometimes there is a thin line between success and failure. You have to be careful not to become complacent.'

He is also a firm believer in playing fair. He says: 'I have always been very straight in my dealings with people and that is very important to me. I haven't trodden on anyone to get here. That's a nice feeling.'

23

Mark Wilkinson
Founder of Mark Wilkinson Furniture

Mark Wilkinson did not have an easy time at school. He was severely dyslexic, but it was the 1950s and nobody could understand what was wrong with him, so his condition went undiagnosed. As a result he spent most of his time staring out of the window. Nor did he find much support for his difficulties at home, a council house in Buckinghamshire. 'My parents were fearsomely clever people, but they were also frustrated intellectually,' he says. 'They would have loved to have gone to university. I was obviously smart, so when I didn't come home with good results they used to get cross with me. They were disappointed that I was not some form of achiever because they wanted that for themselves.'

He was encouraged to sing by a music teacher at school, and at the age of 13 was good enough to be offered a place at the London School of Music. But his family advised him to turn it down because they did not think he would be able to cope.

Wilkinson's time at school was not entirely wasted, however. While staring out of the window he gradually taught himself the art of looking at objects in a completely different way. He says: 'I spent a lot of time changing the geography around me and visually playing with the environment, moving tractors and hedges and trees round. It wasn't until I was in my mid-thirties that I realised it wasn't something that everybody could do.'

Happily, he was taken under the wing of the crafts master who persuaded his other teachers to let him work alone at the back of his class. Wilkinson made stained-glass windows and carved things from wood while other lessons went on around him. He says: 'I owe a lot to my crafts master. He understood what made me tick and he believed in me completely.'

Wilkinson also began to spend his evenings and weekends helping to make furniture with his father and grandfather, who were both carpenters. When he left school at the age of 14 without any qualifications and hardly able to read or write, he realised it was something that suited him. He says: 'I learnt that if I wanted to be accepted and not be called thick and stupid, as I was at school, then the way lay in making things beautiful. Since then making things beautiful has almost been a neurotic compulsion. It is something that gives me great solace.'

By the age of 19 Wilkinson was good enough to be offered a place at college in High Wycombe to study furniture making. Once again, however, he turned it down – this time because he did not think he was good enough and was frightened of failure. Instead, when his parents moved to Somerset, he went with them and, on impulse, bought a derelict nine-bedroom monastery. Because he had no money of his own, he did a deal with the woman who sold it to him to pay her the money in instalments.

Wilkinson renovated the monastery with the help of friends and then rented out rooms to them. He says: 'I was the richest hippy around. We used to race around the countryside advertising for Baby Belling cookers. It was great fun.' He also started up a workshop in the garden of the monastery, where he began making wooden doors and windows for local building companies.

Wilkinson abandoned his craft for a couple of years while he went to live in a squat in south London and work for a

Fact file

Date of birth: 25 October 1950

Marital status: married with two children

Highest level of education achieved: secondary school

Qualifications: fellow of Chartered Society of Designers, member of Mensa

Interests: learning to horse ride, scuba diving, motorcycling, clay pigeon shooting, cooking

Personal philosophy: 'It is important to live life according to a moral code.'

charity, but returned to set up a furniture workshop with a couple of friends. It was the late 1970s, the dawn of the era of stripped pine, Laura Ashley and Welsh dressers. Wilkinson quickly found a demand for his individually designed, hand-built wooden furniture. He says: 'Furniture is my way of speaking. I just took the feeling and the temperature of the time and translated it into a furniture style that people could read and understand. It was about singing a song and making a statement.'

His big break came when he was asked to design a kitchen in old pine for the wife of record producer Chris Wright, the owner of Chrysalis records. Word spread and suddenly Wilkinson found himself swamped with orders. So in 1978 he and his friends founded the Smallbone company, and soon developed a strong following for their individually hand-crafted kitchens. Four years later, however, he decided to leave Smallbone and start up on his own again. 'I had lost the space to move and breathe and had become constrained. I am best unfettered. I was instantly happier,' he says.

Wilkinson now runs his own company, which designs bespoke kitchens, bedrooms and bathrooms. He has also just launched a range of paints and a collection of boxes, bowls and trays. His company, Mark Wilkinson Furniture, in which he has a 65 per cent stake, has 270 employees and in 2004 will have sales of £20 million.

Now 54, Wilkinson admits that throughout his life he has always been driven by fear: 'My motivation is fear of failure, every time. I think if you asked successful entrepreneurs, most would say they are motivated by fear.' He is not, however, remotely interested in money. He says: 'I was brought up as a council-house kid so I know the value of money. I understand what a pound is and what it means to be poor. But I can honestly say I've never done anything for money. I just do what I do, as hard as I can.'

24

Prue Leith
Founder of Leith's

The first time Prue Leith decided to start up her own catering business it survived only a few weeks. 'I had this idea that I could feed actors in their dressing rooms between the matinee and the evening show,' she says. 'I called it Matinee Collations. But I didn't realise that most actors don't like to eat between shows. They prefer to walk in the park or go to the pub. Then I would arrive with the few orders I'd got, only to find that the play had folded and no one was there. It was hopeless.' Happily her second attempt at starting a business worked rather better. Indeed she eventually sold the catering company, restaurant and cooking school she had created for a sum believed to be £10 million.

Brought up in South Africa, Leith had little interest in cooking as a child because all the food her family ate at home was prepared by their cook. Indeed her first three choices of career were to teach people to ride horses, to become an actress like her mother, or to be a theatre designer. She went to university to study drama and literature, but it was not a success and she dropped out in the

Prue Leith

second year. She says: 'I just kept changing my mind about what I wanted to do. My father was pretty despairing.'

It was not until she went to Paris at the age of 21 to learn French while working as an au pair that she realised she wanted to create good food for a living. She says: 'The woman I worked for would go to one shop to buy croissants, another to buy baguettes and a third to buy gateaux. I thought she was crazy. It had never occurred to me there was such a thing as the best shop for croissants. It was like scales falling from my eyes.'

Sadly just as she had discovered her vocation, her father died. Leith says: 'I think he thought it was just another one of my mad ideas. I would have really liked him to know I finally stopped flapping around.'

She secured a place on the advanced Cordon Bleu course in London by pretending she had already worked in the kitchens of a restaurant. She admits: 'I was entirely economical with the truth. I knew nothing about cooking.' However she managed to pass the course and got a job cooking for a firm of solicitors, where she determinedly worked her way through the *Cordon Bleu* cookery book page by page until one of them begged her to stop. She says: 'Round about August I hit the chicken chapter, so we had chicken every day. I had no idea about menu planning.'

The job led to more work catering for weddings and, despite the failure of Matinee Collations, Leith soon felt brave enough to start up a new catering company, Leith's Good Food. But she still did not have much idea how to run a business. Before she could afford to run a car she transported everything by Underground, and once left a box of live lobsters on the train. Neither were her attempts to hire staff too successful. She says: 'There wasn't enough work for both of us so we played tennis during the day and in the evening I went out to work to pay her wages. It was a disaster.'

Despite the chaotic debut the business thrived, and seven years later Leith opened her restaurant, Leith's, in Notting Hill, with £30,000, of which a third was borrowed from her mother. From the start she adopted a businesslike approach, hiring a chef rather than doing the cooking herself. She says: 'I realised early on that I am not the best cook in the world. But I am very good at hiring good people and creating the right atmosphere for them to do their best.'

Fact file

Date of birth: 18 February 1940

Marital status: widowed with two children

Highest level of education achieved: university (but did not complete course)

Qualifications: First in Matriculation (equivalent to A level); Advanced Cordon Bleu certificate

Interests: tennis, fishing, walking, collecting old china

Personal philosophy: 'Don't spend time with anyone you don't like.'

She also opened a cookery school nearby after realising that she was paying her staff to teach them to cook the way she wanted – and it would make a lot more sense to get people to pay her instead. It was so successful that within a few years it had to move to a bigger building because so many students wanted to take the course.

Not everything Leith touched turned to gold. Her decision to sell the businesses in 1995 was partly because of the failure of her Serpentine restaurant in the middle of Kensington Gardens. It ran up losses of £300,000. 'I was over-confident and did not do enough research,' she says. 'I was convinced that if you gave people a wonderful glass of Chablis and a plate of smoked salmon, they would just flock in. And they did if it was a sunny day, but when it rained nobody came. We lost a lot of money and it shook my confidence.'

Leith happily admits to enjoying making money: 'I used to think that the whole point of being a cook was the satisfaction of making perfect food. Then, when I became more of a businesswoman, I realised there was just as much satisfaction in a perfect profit and loss account. I got a real buzz of pleasure if I looked at the month's figures and had made a lot of money.'

Selling her businesses has not lightened her workload, however. Leith is a non-executive director of Woolworths and Whitbread, has written three novels and chairs several charitable organisations. Now aged 64, she says: 'I just can't resist doing things. If I am interested in something then I always want to get involved. I have avoided being on village committees because I know I would find myself saying, "Oh I'll do that, I'll do that."'

25

Christopher Wray
Founder of Christopher Wray Lighting

When Christopher Wray left school at the age of 17 in 1957 he had big plans to become Britain's youngest professional magician, so he took a job as a clown's assistant in Bridlington and did magic tricks during his show. When the season ended, however, Wray discovered there was not much of a demand for magicians. So he decided to become an actor instead. He moved down to London from Yorkshire where he was bought up and managed to get a place at stage school. Then he landed parts in television shows such as *Upstairs Downstairs* and *Doctor Who* before joining a repertory company touring Ireland.

It was Wray's job to scour junk shops for props for the show, and while he was looking he started buying bits of bric-a-brac for himself at the same time. So when an actors' strike made it difficult to get work back in London, a friend suggested he hire a stall in the newly opened Chelsea Antique Market. He could sell the things he had collected as a way of making money until the strike ended. Wray says: 'I

didn't know anything about this business so I just put everything I had on the stall and put a price on it.'

The first thing he sold was a Victorian paraffin oil lamp. So he quickly bought more from nearby junk shops, where they had ended up after being discarded as houses in rural parts of the UK were fitted with electric lights. He polished them up and put them on his stall, and when they sold straight away too, for several times what he had paid for them, Wray started specialising in old oil lamps. One of his regular suppliers was a man who would drive up from Somerset each week with dozens of them in the back of an old camper van. Wray says: 'I never deliberately thought about going into lighting. It was pure luck really.'

He had run the stall for a year when he discovered that a post office on Chelsea's King's Road was closing down. So he borrowed £1,000 from his mother and reopened the post office as a specialist lighting shop, renting it for £750 a year and getting a friend to look after it whenever he got acting jobs.

Wray's timing was perfect. It was 1964 and the King's Road was about to become the epicentre of the swinging sixties. Actor Dudley Moore would come in to play the harmonium Wray kept in the shop.

In the first week Wray sold enough lamps to pay a year's rent. He says: 'One customer just went round the shop and bought all the best lamps. I couldn't believe it. I had to rush out and buy more things to sell.' But his dual life could not last. When Wray was offered a permanent part as the village policeman in the television soap *Emmerdale Farm*, he realised he had to choose between acting and his lighting business. He chose the latter. He says: 'Acting was a wonderful life but I realised I had a unique thing here. And as an actor you never really make any money.'

The shop continued to do well. When customers started asking for replacement glass shades for their lamps because the original shades were hard to find, Wray persuaded a factory in Yorkshire to make new shades from original moulds. He also got a factory in Birmingham to make replacement brass parts for lamps. As demand grew he expanded by buying up shops as they came up for sale around his own. At one stage he owned 10 shops on the same street.

Wray eventually realised, however, it would make a lot more sense to have one large, purpose-built shop. So in

Fact file

Date of birth: 8 March 1940

Marital Status: married with three children

High level of education achieved: boarding school

Qualifications: four O levels

Interests: classic car rallying, water sports

Personal philosophy: 'Always look on the bright side of life.'

1983 he bought some land from the local gas board and after several complicated property transactions and much negotiating with the bank, finally opened the doors of his new shop seven years later in 1990. He says: 'It was my dream to build the absolute ultimate lighting emporium. It was designed so that the whole of the top floor is my office. I am king up there.'

This time, however, his timing was not so good. The new shop opened for business just as recession hit. He says: 'It was as though the sky had fallen in. We looked at each other and said, where has everybody gone?' Wray took immediate action by bringing out a catalogue aimed specifically at retail customers, which highlighted the less expensive items in his shop. Happily it worked and the business survived. The company now has 17 outlets in the UK and a franchise operation in Japan. It sells more than 4,000 types of lights, employs 180 people, and in 2004 will have sales of £8 million.

Indeed the name Christopher Wray has become so synonymous with lighting that many customers are surprised to discover that Christopher Wray is a real person. He says: 'People are always coming up to me and saying, "Oh you do exist, do you?" They just assume it is a fictitious name.'

Wray says the secret of his success has been finding something he enjoys doing: 'It is about wanting to succeed and having the courage of your convictions. But the overriding thing is that it is such fun.'

Now 63, Wray has no plans to retire. 'I don't see the point,' he says. 'Some people tell me I'm mad and that I should have sold the business so I wouldn't have all this hassle. But the hassle is part of what I do and I get great satisfaction out of it. I am always thinking of the business. I wake up in the night and have to write little notes.'

26

Heather Gilchrist
Founder of Happitots

For many entrepreneurs the hardest part of setting up their own businesses is coping with the financial aspects, but for former nurse Heather Gilchrist by far the biggest headache in launching her chain of children's nurseries was having to deal with staff. She says: 'When I started I naively thought that if I was nice to people and treated them really well, they would be happy. In the early days, if someone left because they didn't like the job or they weren't happy, I used to take it personally and get really upset about it. But I learnt that you can't make everybody happy all the time.'

She also found it extremely lonely being the boss. 'When I was a nurse I was part of a team and would go out drinking with my colleagues from work,' she says, 'but I realised that I couldn't be one of the girls any more. They don't want me to go out for a drink with them because I am the boss. It has taken me a long time to get used to that. It's really hard because I am a friendly person and there are lots of staff I think I could be really good friends with.'

Gilchrist hit on the idea of opening a nursery when her son Thomas was born. She started looking for a place in a

nursery for him in Edinburgh where they lived. But she quickly discovered she had left it far too late and that only the worst nurseries still had places available. So Gilchrist decided to start one of her own. She says: 'There was a demand for quality and I knew I could do better than a lot of other nurseries I had seen. I can be pretty determined once I have decided what I want to do. So I got in touch with the relevant official bodies and found out exactly what the requirements were.'

However, finding suitable premises was a lot harder than she expected. She bought a street map of Edinburgh and marked on it where every existing nursery in the city was located. Then she went to talk to estate agents in the areas which she felt needed one. But that was where the problems began. 'I knew exactly how many square feet I needed, but nobody took me seriously,' she says. 'It was horrendous. I think if I had been in a pinstripe suit and spoken in a posh accent, it might have been a bit easier.'

In desperation, she spent hours driving round in her car with her baby by her side looking for something suitable. Eventually, a friend spotted an empty church building and called her. As soon as Gilchrist saw it, she realised it was exactly what she wanted. She bought the building for £90,000, paying for it with £20,000 raised from remortgaging her flat and £70,000 borrowed from the bank. Six months later she opened for business.

It was hard work at the beginning. She had so little spare cash she could not afford to buy a washing machine or a dryer for the nursery, and had to take all the dirty laundry home each night. But she did not have a dryer there either and so would have to drape wet sheets and towels around the house.

Fortunately Gilchrist was used to dealing with challenging situations. Brought up in Cheshire, she trained as a nurse after leaving school and then went straight to Papua New Guinea for two years to work with the Red Cross. After that she spent five years in Australia nursing AIDS and HIV patients. She returned to Britain because her mother had breast cancer. She had planned to stay only briefly but while in this country she fell in love with a man she met and decided to stay.

Gilchrist opened her first nursery in Edinburgh in 1996 and it did so well that two years later she opened a second

Fact file

Date of birth: 15 April 1962

Marital status: married with one child

Highest level of education achieved: secondary school

Qualifications: six O levels, one A level, registered general nurse

Interests: going to the gym, socialising, theatre, reading

Personal philosophy: 'Live for the moment. Don't put off anything you can do today.'

one in Glasgow. When that went well, too, she opened more. However, she soon discovered that the parents and staff at her first nursery found it difficult to accept her changed role. She says: 'Because it was my first nursery the staff had been used to seeing me there every day. Then all of a sudden I wasn't there all the time because the business was growing. But staff and parents still expected me to be there all the time and would be asking why I wasn't coming in. I was getting really stressed about the situation. And I couldn't be businesslike about it because it was my first nursery and I was very attached to it emotionally. So I had to sell it. I needed to let go of the first one in order to move on.'

Gilchrist now owns 12 Happitots nurseries throughout Scotland, which between them cater for 2,000 children of up to five years old. She also recently opened a training division to train nursery staff. In 2004 her turnover is expected to be £3 million.

Now aged 42, she says she has always been driven by a desire to show she could make a success of her venture. She says: 'I wanted to prove to myself and my family that I could do it. At the beginning it was difficult to get people to take me seriously, but nowadays it is great because people tell me about which buildings are available for my next nursery. I wouldn't have ever believed I could do this. Now if anyone tells me they want to do something, I always tell them to go for it.'

27

Richard Beggs
Founder of Moving Venue Group

Richard Beggs always dreamt of becoming the manager of a large hotel. After spending every summer working in tourist hotels in his hometown of Weymouth, Dorset, he left school at 16 to do a four-year apprenticeship with the Savoy Hotel group. He says: 'I was hell-bent on becoming a hotshot hotel manager working in a corporate environment.'

When he got a job as the manager of the Dover Street wine bar in London's Mayfair, however, he began to think his future might lie in other directions. He started organising parties for customers and soon discovered he really enjoyed it. When he was asked to organise the opening of a big furniture showroom it went so well that, in 1984 and at the age of 26, he decided to leave his job to set up his own catering and event management company.

He says: 'I suddenly realised this was a formula for a very successful business and knew I wanted to pursue it further. By being in a less bureaucratic environment I could have a greater influence over decisions.'

He funded the start-up of his business with savings of £3,000 which he had been intending to use as the deposit on a flat. Instead he moved in with his girlfriend and used the money to get a £10,000 overdraft facility from the bank.

His decision to go it alone did not, however, get whole-hearted approval from his family and friends.

He says: 'The Dover Street wine bar was packed out every night. Everyone thought I was completely round the twist walking away from that.'

Just three months after he opened for business, though, Beggs struck lucky. He was cold-called by an insurance agent who hoped to sell him some insurance. Beggs agreed to meet him on the condition the agent introduced him to some of his clients.

As a result, Beggs landed a huge contract to organise a social programme for a group of businessmen in London for a conference.

He says: 'That was what really put me on the map. I had been organising events for £500 and £600 a time and suddenly here was a £30,000 piece of business.'

Not every venture went as smoothly, however. When Beggs was asked to organise a party to launch British Caledonian's inaugural flight from London to New York, his team had the inspired idea of holding it in an art gallery and decorating the walls with an exhibition of paintings of New York. But when the paintings arrived they turned out to be of Paris. So Beggs and his colleagues had to rush out and spend a fortune buying posters of Manhattan and getting them framed. He says: 'We were still nailing things together as the first guests were arriving.'

Then in 1989 recession struck and overnight demand for events management dried up. The situation was made worse by the fact that Beggs had invested heavily in commercial property.

He says: 'I thought the best way forward was to buy premises rather than have enormous exposure to big rents on offices. But it was almost as if I was signing on the dotted line and Margaret Thatcher was shouting, "Right, you can start the recession now, he has just put pen to paper." We owed the bank £500,000 and it was evident our bankers had lost confidence in us.'

Fact file

Date of birth: 18 September 1957

Marital status: married with one child

Highest level of education achieved: secondary school

Qualifications: CSE Grade 1 in Art, professional degree from the hotel, catering and international management association

Interests: marathon running, playing with son

Personal philosophy: 'If you see your ship coming in, swim out and meet it. If you can see an opportunity, seize it.'

The day before the staff Christmas party his lawyer advised him that the only way out was to go into voluntary liquidation. But Beggs refused. He says: 'It would have meant taking a lot of people out with me because my suppliers would have got hit at a time when none of them could handle it. I just felt it would be the most shitty thing to do.' Instead he arranged a meeting with his bank. He says: 'I went in there thinking I have got to give the pitch of a lifetime. I was terrified. I put the keys on the table and said, there they are if you want them, but if you are prepared to let me carry on working then I will repay the debt.'

The bank reluctantly allowed him three months to get the business back on track. Beggs immediately shifted the focus toward organising events for clients he thought would do best in a recession, such as bankers and lawyers. The business survived.

When Sydney was unveiled as the venue for the 2000 Olympic Games, Beggs decided it could be the opportunity he had been waiting for to turn his company into an international player. He realised there would be a huge demand for conferences in Sydney in the run-up to the games – and that his company had just the experience to organise them. Within two months of the announcement he had invested £10,000 to set up an office in Australia, using the services of a former employee who had recently emigrated there.

He says: 'I wanted to make a statement. I thought it was time we elevated ourselves out of the small-business scenario and showed our clients we were up for the long haul.' The gamble paid off. Beggs quickly won work organising conferences for companies hoping to get contracts for the Olympic Games. Then later his company won work organising big parties to celebrate the completion of those contracts.

Today the firm is regarded as one of Australia's leading event management companies, and Beggs has been appointed a member of a panel set up to advise British businesses of the potential commercial value of London's bid to stage the 2012 Olympic Games. His company, which he wholly owns, is worth £4 million and in 2004 will have a turnover of £8 million. Beggs, now 47, says: 'There is an element of entrepreneurial flair in everybody. The more of it you can apply and use, the more successful you will become.'

28

Duncan Bannatyne
Founder of Bannatyne Leisure

Duncan Bannatyne was lying on a beach in Jersey with his girlfriend when he realised it was time to do something with his life. He was 30, penniless, and had spent the previous five years working as a barman and having a great social life. He says: 'I suddenly realised I was the oldest swinger in town. So I said to my girlfriend, let's go back to the mainland, start a business and become millionaires.'

The only problem was how to go about it. Brought up in a poor area of Glasgow, Bannatyne left school at 15 without qualifications to join the Royal Navy. He then worked on farms as a fitter and welder. His only aim in life was to make sure he did not follow in the footsteps of his family. 'My father, my sister, my uncle and my cousins all worked in the Singer sewing machine factory,' Bannatyne says. 'The bell would go at six o'clock and they would all come out like zombies. I knew I didn't want to work there. And I didn't want to be poor.'

On his return from Jersey Bannatyne got a job in a bakery, and to make ends meet also bought used cars at auction to do up and sell on. When an ice-cream van came

up for sale he bought it for £450 and quit his job. He saved every penny he made selling ice creams to buy more vans, until two years later he had a fleet of six and was making £70,000 a year. But there was a problem. He says: 'I put on a lot of weight. I was more than 16 stone because I was eating ice cream all the time.'

He decided he needed a change of direction, so he sold the business and started buying terraced houses to provide accommodation for the unemployed instead. When a newspaper article highlighting the shortage of nursing homes caught his eye, however, he decided to invest everything he had to build one of his own.

Bannatyne says: 'I went round local nursing homes and found old ladies living eight to a room at the top of flights of stairs. The government was paying a lot of money to house them. I calculated that if I built a nursing home with 30 single bedrooms I would fill mine, and the others would close down because I would be offering better accommodation at the same price. And I would still be making whacking great money. And that was what happened. It was full within three months.'

He footed the £180,000 cost of building the home by selling his house, car and everything he had. He also managed to borrow a total of £40,000 from four different credit cards after the bank refused his request for a loan. 'I went to the bank manager at Barclays and said here's my projections, this is phenomenal, I have got to do this, lend me some money. But he said that if it was that good, everybody would be doing it – and he threw me out of his office.' But Bannatyne had the last laugh. As soon as his nursing home opened for business it was valued at £650,000 and he was able to remortgage it to pay off his debts.

The same day he started building an 18-bedroom extension, and within weeks had bought land to build a second nursing home. He kept building more nursing homes until by 1992 he had a chain of 30. But he also had personal debts of £6 million and the strain was beginning to show. Bannatyne started falling asleep in the middle of conversations and would have to pull over while driving. He says: 'The specialist said I was under pressure and so my mind was switching off as a release. I realised that I was under stress.'

Fortunately it was not for long. Within a few months he had floated the company, Quality Care Homes, on the stock

Fact file

Date of birth: 2 February 1949

Marital status: divorced, six children

High level of education achieved: secondary school

Qualifications: none

Interests: socialising, working out at the gym, spending time with his children

Personal philosophy: 'Life is a bowl of cherries – just watch out for the pips.'

market and was able to pay off all his debts and pocket £1 million for himself.

Suddenly he was chairman of a public company with a 73 per cent stake, which with his salary gave him £250,000 a year. But Bannatyne soon became bored working in an office and in 1997 sold the company for £46 million, giving him a personal windfall of £26 million.

He decided to use some of the money to build a chain of nursery schools, starting with one in his home town of Darlington, after realising he was having to drive 10 miles to take his daughter to nursery school each day. He also decided to open a gym in Darlington after he broke his leg skiing and realised that the nearest gym he could use to improve his muscles was many miles from home too.

Bannatyne sold his chain of nursery schools, Just Learning, in 2001 for £22 million. His 30-strong nationwide chain of gyms, Bannatyne Leisure, is expected to make profits of £5.2 million in 2004 after generating sales of £30.2 million. He is now planning to open a chain of casinos, and has been granted a licence to open his first premises in Newcastle in 2005. He admits: 'I get bored very easily and so what ever business I have got, I am always looking for something else to do.'

Bannatyne, 45, now has a personal fortune of more than £115 million. He says: 'The secret of being successful in business is that there is no secret. Anybody with any spark of intelligence in this country can become a millionaire. You just have to work very hard.'

29

Angela Wright

Founder of Crealy Adventure Park

Angela Wright had to get pretty good at tidying her bedroom when she was a child.

She was brought up at Hayes Barton farm in east Devon, the birthplace of Sir Walter Raleigh, and every afternoon her parents would show visitors round the house for 20p a time. She says: 'Every day at two o'clock it would be, oh my goodness the visitors are coming up the path, quick go and tidy your room. Sometimes I would be too late so I would have to hide things under the bed.'

As she grew older, Wright earned pocket money by serving cream teas to visitors on the lawn. She says: 'I only realised with hindsight that it was a really wonderful, magical childhood. I could make dens in the barns and climb the trees and run wild over the common. And yet it was a safe adventure because it was cocooned.' The memory stayed with her after she left home to go travelling and then work nearby as a secretary. When her parents bought a farm of their own in Devon she decided to recreate the magic of her childhood by turning it into an adventure park. She says: 'I wanted to

provide somewhere where families could have a really magical day and children could realise their own capabilities and courage through adventure play.'

It was a bold plan. Wright had just had her first child and had no experience of running a business. She spent six months researching the idea before plucking up the courage to even suggest it to her parents. She says: 'Their initial reaction was it would be too much to take on. They thought it would be very daunting and they didn't know if it would work.' In the end it took Wright a further 12 months of research before she was able to convince her family to provide the financial backing for the park.

She says: 'I had to draw up a very solid business plan for my family to want to get involved, not just financially but also from a lifestyle perspective. I remember telling them I would make sure they wouldn't have to work any harder.' But there were still hurdles to overcome. The Highways Department refused to allow her to create an access to the adventure park from the main road. When it finally agreed, it was on the condition that Wright build a turning bay and entrance at a cost of £70,000. The only way she could justify the expense was to go back to the drawing board and find a way of accommodating more visitors.

Crealy Adventure Park finally opened for business in 1989. It was divided into six areas to suit different age groups, including an animal realm where children can hold newborn chicks and feed lambs, and another area with family rides. It reached its target of 40,000 visitors in the first year of operation and moved into profit in year three. In 2001, however, the business faced the prospect of ruin with the onset of foot-and-mouth disease. While the park itself was not directly affected, visitor numbers fell by a fifth, which had a devastating effect on profits. Wright responded by diversifying into corporate hospitality, but it was a fraught time.

She says: 'It was a real disaster. We didn't know what would happen or how much our business would be affected. A lot of lateral thinking went on. It really made us look at our business and remember that crises can come out of nowhere and that it is really important to protect what you have.' Visitor numbers gradually recovered, and the park now attracts 500,000 people a year, and is expected to generate a turnover of more than £5 million in 2004.

Fact file

Date of birth: 20 January 1962

Marital status: married with five children

Highest level of education achieved: secondary school

Qualifications: eight O levels

Interests: spending time with family, travel, reading, and politics

Personal philosophy: 'Be too busy to have time for regrets. And always look for the best in people.'

Early in 2004 Wright also added a second park to the business, buying the former Shires Family Adventure Park in Cornwall for several million pounds and reopening it in April as Cornwall's Crealy Great Adventure Park. It currently has 175,000 visitors a year. She also decided that instead of just having a five-year business plan for the company, she would have a 25-year plan. She explains: 'During an appraisal a member of staff told me that having a five-year business plan was all very well, but that Crealy was her career and so she wanted to know what I was going to be doing in 25 years' time. Initially I thought oh no, but it has been really interesting to do. And I always think that until you have something written down, you can't improve on it because ideas in your head are too ephemeral.'

Despite the company's expanding size Wright's family are still very much involved in running the business. Her father is chairman, her mother is a director and involved with the buying, her brother is finance director and her husband is in charge of running the new park in Cornwall. Wright herself is managing director.

Wright, who now has five children of her own aged between 5 and 18, says: 'I feel fortunate to be able to deliver some of the most memorable moments in children's lives. When I see a child walking across an aerial walkway or holding a chick, that's quite special.' She says getting her whole family involved in realising her dream has driven her determination to make the business a success: 'It has been a real privilege to work with my family. But I do feel a lot of responsibility to make the business work because they trusted me and jumped on board with me. I would still have started my own business, but it would have been very different. I would not have achieved what I have and I can't imagine that it would have been as rewarding.'

30

Daniel Mitchell
Founder of The Source

Daniel Mitchell has never let a lack of money get in the way of starting his own business.

Brought up in Southend-on-Sea by one parent, he began his first company, selling office equipment, at the age of 19. He funded it entirely on the back of credit from suppliers after he discovered he could pay them 30 days after customers had paid him.

Unfortunately, his entire experience of business at that point consisted of 18 months of selling equipment for someone else. Mitchell had no real idea about how to run a company, and after two years his firm went bust. He says: 'I decided I could do a much better job of it myself, but I quickly learnt that I couldn't. Looking back at it now, I can't believe I managed to keep it going for as long as I did. I didn't really have a business plan and I didn't understand cash flow. Everything was worked out on the back of a cigarette packet.'

Mitchell was still determined to have a company of his own, however, and so he took a job with a finance firm in London to find out how businesses actually worked. 'I went on training courses to find out how to read a balance sheet

and learn about the importance of cashflow,' he says. 'It really gave me a good insight into how a company ticks financially and I discovered it was something that really interested me.'

After spending a year travelling round America, at the age of 23 Mitchell decided that it was time to try again. So in 1993 he set up a company selling computer parts to maintenance companies. He explains: 'I had a reasonable understanding of the IT market and I knew that in order to be successful a business either had to be huge or it had to be niche. So I chose a relatively high-margin niche market.' Once again he did it without having to find any cash upfront, negotiating a three-month rent-free deal on premises and then trading on suppliers' credit and borrowing on his credit cards to fill the gaps where necessary. He says: 'There was no capital involved in the business. It was simply a matter of starting trading and getting suppliers' credit and then reinvesting the profit.'

He quickly realised he had discovered an untapped demand and sales took off. But after five years of strong growth, averaging 35 per year a year, in 1998 Mitchell realised that the market's low barriers to entry left his company increasingly vulnerable to competition. 'I just couldn't see how I could build up the kind of business that I wanted to build up in the next five years in that particular marketplace,' he says. 'There were very few barriers to stop my sales manager going round the corner with a credit card and an overdraft and setting up in competition to me.'

As he looked around for what to do next, he suddenly realised that the perfect opportunity lay right on his doorstep. 'We had handled the insurance claims for a couple of small clients, so it got me thinking about what actually happens when an insurance company gets a claim for a computer,' he says. 'I rang up an insurance company and asked if it would be interested in something that took away the hassle of validating claims and supplying the computer equipment. The answer was yes. So I rang up four other insurance companies and it was exactly the same story.' Inspired by his discovery, Mitchell decided to set up a business that handled claims on behalf of insurance companies by validating the claim and then repairing or replacing the damaged equipment.

The business, which he called The Source, went so well that after a year Mitchell brought in business angels to

Fact file

Date of birth: 13 August 1969

Marital status: married with two children

Highest level of education achieved: sixth form college

Qualifications: four A levels

Interests: motor racing, playing squash, skiing

Personal philosophy: 'Everything is possible. It is just a question of figuring out how.'

invest £500,000 in the company. By the end of 2000 it was generating far more income than the original parts business. It was, however, a frustrating time. He says: 'I was doing loads of administration and working lots of hours because I couldn't afford to employ someone to do the administrative things that needed to be done. But it was an absolute waste of my time because I wasn't adding value to the business. I would have grown the business much quicker if I had hired someone to help.'

He eventually realised that the solution was to employ a chief executive who had been a director on the board of an FTSE 100 company. It was a sound move. Mitchell says: 'It has freed me up to be more strategic and more customer facing, which is what I am good at. It has also brought a wealth of experience as the business grows. If I had my time again, I would have spent more money on recruiting people earlier than I did. Success is about customers – but it is also about the people that you employ.'

In 2001 he decided to sell a majority stake in the original parts business to concentrate on growing The Source, which in 2004 is expected to make sales of £35 million. Mitchell, now 35, says: 'There are two things that make me go into work in the morning. First, I have to enjoy what I am doing and get a buzz from it and it has to be an intellectual challenge. The second is getting a financial reward from doing the things I do. I think you make your own luck. I am an absolute believer that the harder I work, the luckier I get. I tend to focus on the positive. I don't really listen to people saying no. I just work out a different way of doing something.'

31

Emma Bridgewater
Founder of Bridgewater Pottery

Becoming a ceramics designer was not the most obvious way for Emma Bridgewater to make her fortune. She confesses to being hopeless at making pottery and she has never had any formal training in design. Not that any of this seems to have done her much harm. Her company, which is perhaps best known for its collections of plates and bowls with writing around the sides, has established an individual niche within the ceramics market and in the process has become a hugely successful enterprise.

For many years Bridgewater had no idea what she wanted to do as a career and was extremely envious of those who did. She says: 'I longed for a vocation and to know what I was going to be. I was so jealous of people who knew from an early age that they wanted to be ballet dancers or gymnasts or whatever.' She left university with a degree in English literature still no clearer, but got a job with a knitwear company after meeting the owner at a party. She says: 'They were run off their feet because the Princess of Wales had worn one of their jumpers with a sheep design on it and everyone wanted one. So I offered to help.'

While she was there Bridgewater asked dozens of questions about how the business worked. By the time she left 18 months later she was convinced that what she really wanted to do was start her own business. But she still had no idea what her business would actually do. Then one day she was searching the shops for cups and saucers to give her mother as a birthday present. When she could not find anything she liked, she decided to design some herself.

She went back to the family home to study her mother's existing collection of crockery, and realised that those she liked had been decorated using sponge printing, a traditional technique by which simple designs are applied to ceramics using sponges. She says: 'I looked at the old pieces and thought, this is perfect for me.' She sketched a mug, dish and bowl on a piece of paper and then paid a potter in Stoke-on-Trent £500 to make 100 unglazed pieces from her drawings. Then she took them back to her flat in London and started experimenting, creating her own shapes and then applying them with sponges.

She says: 'I think if I had been to art school I would have been discouraged or told it was impossible. But instead I just filled a dustbin with glaze in the bathroom and stirred it with a great big stick. I was endlessly rubbing off the designs and starting again because I couldn't afford to waste any pots.'

After three months Bridgewater had created four designs and sent a finished bowl or mug to 120 retail buyers accompanied by a brief description of the pattern. She was so confident of success she deliberately priced her pieces at twice that of her competitors. It was a risky move, but the gamble worked.

Harrods, John Lewis and the General Trading Company immediately placed orders and Bridgewater Pottery was born. And thanks to the hefty price, orders were kept at a level she could cope with. She says: 'The price made the buyers nervous. But I never had any doubts because it instinctively felt right. It set a new benchmark in the industry and helped keep the volume down, which in retrospect was essential.'

Determined that her crockery would not look like something from a craft fair, Bridgewater also decided to get it all

Fact file

Date of birth: 23 December 1960

Marital status: married with four children

Highest educational level achieved: university

Qualifications: BA (Hons) in English Literature from London University

Interests: picnicking and cooking outdoors, gardening, spending time with her children

Personal philosophy: 'The worst thing you can do is hesitate. Get on with things even if you haven't fully worked out how to do them, because even the worst case scenario may turn out to be better than you expect.'

made in a factory in the traditional Potteries area of Stoke on Trent. At the beginning she delivered each order herself in a rented van, but with no money to invest in the business, cash flow was precarious. She survived only by getting her pots on 30 days' credit and persuading buyers to pay her in 28 days. But then crisis hit. One day she turned up to find the factory on the brink of liquidation. She had just two days to find the money to buy the factory and save her business, and managed it only by borrowing heavily from her family.

Business boomed and when Bridgewater wanted to take time out to have children she brought in managers to run the company in her absence. She says it was a big mistake. Sales stagnated at £2 million and profits declined. She says: 'With hindsight, I didn't communicate my ideas properly to the managers. I gave them an almost impossible task. I would ask in an agitated way why the business wasn't growing but the systems were so chaotic I could never really find the answer.' So two years ago Bridgewater decided to take back control, getting rid of five people and cutting delivery times from 12 weeks to four.

She admits: 'I had allowed myself to be sidelined. We were ignoring our successes and thrashing around after failures. I realised there was only room for one amateur in the company – and that was me.' Her hands-on approach paid off. The company is now expected to achieve sales of £8 million for 2004.

Bridgewater says she has found running her own business both exhilarating and exhausting: 'It gives you terrific financial freedom if you can make it work. But it is really obsessive. You find yourself talking about it to people at dinner. There's something always just disappearing over the horizon – and you are always galloping madly towards it.'

32

Gerry Pack
Founder of Holiday Extras

Gerry Pack had been working for the same company, Saga Holidays, ever since leaving school and after 14 years he was beginning to wonder where his life was heading. He was 30 years old, had virtually no formal qualifications and knew it would not be easy to find another job where he lived in Folkestone. Then one day Pack's boss asked him to look at how the company dealt with customers who needed overnight stays in airport hotels. When Pack discovered that the existing system was completely unwieldy and was costing Saga a lot of money, he had a sudden inspiration. He says: 'I thought that if we were doing that badly even though we had been selling holidays since 1955, then what was everyone else doing? So I rang some travel agents I knew and asked them how they booked airport hotel rooms for customers.'

It was a revelation. He says: 'I discovered that the only thing the agents had in common was they all hated doing it. They usually had to ring lots of hotels before they found a room, and often bookings went wrong because the prices the hotels charged were always different. And they hardly

ever received commission. So I thought there could be an opportunity here. I could devise a win–win–win formula.'

Pack's big idea was to set himself up as a hotel-room wholesaler, getting advance allocations of rooms from hotels at a large discount and then selling them on to travel agents at a higher price. The hotel would benefit by getting new business, the travel agent would benefit from a simple booking service that was free and paid commission, and the customer would benefit by getting cheaper hotel rooms.

He took some room allocations from hotels at Heathrow, Gatwick and Luton airports. Then he asked a friend who owned a publishing company to join him, and together they devised a clever plan to keep start-up costs to a minimum. The fledging business, Apple Booking Company, would share the same office and the same first name as the publishing company, Apple Communications, so existing staff could answer the phone for both. In return Pack would pay his friend 50p for every booking made.

Pack says: 'The great thing was that if we didn't do any business, we didn't have any costs. I couldn't afford to employ someone to sit there and wait for the phone to ring.'

In fact he managed to start the business with just £100, which he spent on getting some leaflets printed and preparing a marketing plan.

A few days after the first leaflets were sent out to travel agents Pack called the office to see if they had had any impact. He says: 'The lady in the office said we'd had six bookings. I can still remember that moment. I was at my parents house and I started leaping round their front room because I knew then that it was going to work.'

The phones kept on ringing and in the first year the Apple Booking Company sold 4,000 hotel rooms, helped by Pack's decision to have a freephone number. He says: 'It cost us a fortune but it was important for us to be able to tell travel agents that when they made a booking with us it would not cost them anything.' It was, however, harder than he expected to persuade travel agents to switch to using his system. Pack says: 'The phone should have been ringing off the wall because it was such a good idea. But it is extremely difficult to change people's habits and we would go back week after week just reminding them we were there.' Indeed, at first Pack could not afford to give up his old job at Saga and so continued to work there for more

Fact file

Date of birth: 23 May 1953

Marital status: married with four children

Highest level of education achieved: grammar school

Qualifications: two O levels

Interests: playing tennis, golf, hunting, skiing, reading, watching films, great wines

Personal philosophy: 'Make the most of every opportunity. Remember that your destiny is the result of your actions.'

than a year, keeping his fledgling business secret from colleagues, and doing the accounts and paperwork for Apple Booking Company in the evening and at weekends. His double life only ended when his boss at Saga asked him to look after its travel-agent business. Pack realised he faced a conflict of interest and left to work for Apple full-time.

The company was soon doing enough business to be able to afford to move into offices of its own. It gradually added more hotels and then travel insurance, airport car parks and airport lounges to the extras it sold. Pack admits, however, to making some expensive mistakes along the way. Seven years ago he bought a company that organised truck expeditions to Africa and spent £1 million in two years upgrading it before he had to shut it down. He says: 'My problem was that I wanted it to be done properly. I wanted new Mercedes trucks but the business model wouldn't support it. Our competitors were all operating on a shoestring and we couldn't compete with them. I learnt that one business model doesn't necessarily fit all businesses. Some businesses need to operate in different ways.'

Fortunately the core business has thrived, and in 2004 the company, renamed Holiday Extras, celebrated its 21st birthday. It now sells 400,000 rooms a year and in 2004 it is expected to have sales of £92 million. Pack says the secret of his success has been finding something he really enjoys doing: 'When you have a mortgage and children you are driven by money in the sense that you must have a job. But if all you think about is the money, your business is never going to work. You have to be passionate about what you are doing – and you have to want to win.'

33

Zahid Kasim
Founder of Café Lazeez

When Zahid Kasim decided to leave his job at the bank where he had worked for 16 years, he planned to use the money from his severance package to open a restaurant. Unfortunately, the bank he worked for was BCCI and 10 days before he was due to leave, it collapsed. That was the end of Kasim's severance package and all his savings.

Ironically, it was while at BCCI that Kasim had had the idea of opening a restaurant in the first place. As the bank's head of human resources he often had to take people out for lunch, and he soon realised that there were very few high-class Indian restaurants to choose from. Having been born and brought up in Pakistan before his family moved to Britain when he was 10, he felt the absence acutely and thought that there might be room for a new kind of Indian restaurant in the UK. He says: 'I would get pangs for the kind of food I grew up on, but Indian restaurants here were still in the primary stage of evolution. They were still very much first generation. Having Ravi Shankar music playing constantly in the background really didn't do much for me.

I didn't feel it was very relevant. There was this vacuum in the market.'

At the age of 37 with a lifetime spent in the corporate banking world and no money, Kasim was not an obvious candidate to be an entrepreneur. But after the collapse of BCCI, he decided that if he were going to put his plan into action it would have to be now or never. He was offered other jobs in banking, but says: 'I had had enough of banking by that stage and wanted to change direction. I just lost my spirit for the whole thing.'

With no savings to support him, however, he soon realised he needed to enlist the help of his family. And if he was to have any chance of success he needed to get his sister Sabiha, who was a brilliant cook, on board. But Sabiha was busy bringing up three children and already did a lot of corporate entertaining for her husband's colleagues. She did not want to get involved.

In the end it took Kasim nearly two years to persuade her to join him. He says: 'I needed somebody with expertise at a core level, and without her I don't think I would have started this. Eventually she agreed to give me six months to get the foundations sorted, but of course she ended up staying much longer.'

Sabiha's involvement also gave Kasim's family the confidence to provide him with start-up capital of £100,000 in return for equity in the company. As the business grew they took a further stake for £200,000. Kasim admits: 'Persuading them was not that easy but when I got Sabiha on my side we handled it jointly. They knew that Sabiha was a skilled cook and knew about quality control.'

Kasim opened his first Café Lazeez restaurant in 1992 in South Kensington, London. It was not the best of times as Britain was in the middle of a recession. Kasim was determined to make it different from other Indian restaurants, so he hired a designer to give it a minimalist look and deliberately gave no external clues as to the type of food it offered. He even banned the ubiquitous sign hanging in the window of most Indian restaurants at the time, which declared: 'Fully air-conditioned'.

Unfortunately, his ambitious vision initially backfired. He says: 'In the early days people would come in expecting an Italian or French restaurant. They would take one look at the menu and walk straight out. That went on for about six months and it was scary.'

Fact file

Date of birth: 1 January 1954

Marital status: divorced with one child

Highest level of education achieved: university (did not complete course)

Qualifications: three A levels

Interests: listening to music, current affairs

Personal philosophy: 'Inspire to aspire.'

The turning point came when Café Lazeez started attracting the attention of the food critics. One of the first reviews heralded the restaurant as 'the shape of things to come' and soon it was winning awards for its cooking. Kasim says: 'Every week something was written about us saying we were trying to change the whole Indian cuisine context. It was very positive.'

Kasim has now opened three more Café Lazeez restaurants in London and Birmingham, and the business in 2004 will have a turnover of at least £4 million. Right from the start he knew he wanted to create a Café Lazeez brand that could be used in other areas, so in 2001 he opened a fast-food operation called Lazeez Express to provide food at sporting events. He also hopes one day to create a range of food that will be sold in supermarkets.

He says: 'People felt I was crazy because they thought that the brand values created at a high-quality restaurant could not be transposed in this way. But I didn't understand why they couldn't.' In a nice twist he has also embarked on setting up an overseas franchise operation for his restaurants – in Pakistan and India.

Now aged 50, Kasim has no regrets about leaving banking. He says he was never driven by money but instead is really motivated by the thrill of creating something new. 'Money hasn't been a great motivator in my life,' he says. 'For me the most exciting part is creating something that has value. If I can achieve that, then hopefully I will be a happy person. If I can leave something for posterity, that would be fantastic.'

34

Sharon Hilditch
Founder of Crystal Clear

When Sharon Hilditch launched her Crystal Clear skin rejuvenating machine, she decided to ignore conventional ways of marketing a new product such as placing adverts in trade journals. Instead she spent the whole of her first year's promotional budget of £30,000 paying for the services of Max Clifford, the public-relations consultant, in the hope of attracting celebrity followers. It worked. A well-known newsreader was the first to endorse the Crystal Clear treatment. She was soon joined by an actress and a former Page Three girl, generating lots of media coverage and getting the product in front of the public.

Hilditch, 43, says: 'It made a name for us. Trying to educate the customer about a new product can be a struggle, but the more celebrities we got, the more people started asking for Crystal Clear in the salons. And that put pressure on the salons to offer it to their customers.'

Brought up in a working-class area of Liverpool, Hilditch had a difficult start in life. A severe hearing problem in one ear affected her speech development and made it hard to concentrate. She says: 'I struggled at school because I am

not very good when a lot of people are talking around me. The teacher used to shout at me if I used the wrong word.' She nevertheless managed to get her first job at the age of 11 in a hairdresser's by lying about her age. 'My two older sisters had Saturday jobs so I wanted one too,' she says. 'The work ethic was instilled in us from an early age. We knew that if we wanted something we had to go and earn money ourselves to get it.'

She left school at 15 to work in the salon full-time, and two years later bought her own hairdressing salon after her father agreed to act as guarantor for a £8,000 bank loan. The business thrived and Hilditch bought a second salon, but by the time she was 22 she decided it was time to try something else. She had been studying for O and A levels in the evenings at a local college, and decided to take a law degree.

She soon realised, however, that she had to make a choice between law and business. She chose business. Hilditch says: 'To be honest I realised I was making more money than I ever could as a lawyer.' She knew she did not want to go on being a hairdresser, however, and soon sold both salons for a healthy profit.

Her next move was on the other hand not so successful. She invested her entire savings of £30,000 in an advertising sales company, but within a couple of years had lost the lot. She is philosophical about the loss, saying: 'Failure makes you a lot stronger and a lot tougher because you think to yourself, I am never going to be there again.'

Hilditch then took a job in a cosmetic surgery hospital, looking after patients who came in for treatments to ageing skin. She says: 'I really loved coming up with ideas and thinking how we could bring new treatments into the practice. I realised the anti-ageing market was an area I wanted to stay in.' After the surgery, patients needed time to recover, and Hilditch decided there might be a gap in the market for a gentler alternative. She says: 'I wanted to find a method of skin rejuvenation that was not as harsh as the medical techniques but offered more than standard salon treatments.'

She discovered the answer while visiting a dermatologist in Italy – micro-dermabrasion, a method of firing crystals at high pressure to remove layers of dead skin. She says: 'I thought that if I designed a machine that worked at lower pressure and was not so aggressive on the skin, clients could come in once a week for a course of 10 treatments and

Fact file

Date of birth: 21 April 1961

Marital status: long-term partner, two children

Highest level of education achieved: college of further education

Qualifications: one O level, two A levels

Interests: learning to fly a plane, gardening

Personal philosophy: 'You can have anything you want if you want it badly enough.'

get the same effect. The industry was crying out for something new, and salons had started to look at more machine-based treatments, so it was a good time to bring it to the market.'

Hilditch quit her job, and with the help of her partner and some design engineers from Liverpool University spent a year and £30,000 creating a prototype machine and holding clinical trials to ensure the treatment was effective and safe. She finally launched her Crystal Clear machine at a trade show in Manchester in 1995 – and did not sell a thing. But she remained hopeful, saying: 'I knew it would be a success because other exhibitors spent more time on our stand than their own.' She also faced initial scepticism for setting up her skin care company in Liverpool. She says: 'People would always expect us to be either based in London or New York.'

Her optimism paid off and Hilditch now sells more than 1,000 machines a year, of which half are exported. She has also launched a second machine that pushes oxygen and anti-ageing ingredients into the skin, another which provides micro-dermabrasion anti-ageing treatment for hands, and a range of skin-care products. A salon will typically charge clients £35–65 for a 40-minute session on a Crystal Clear machine depending on where it is located, and Crystal Clear sales are expected to reach £5 million for 2004.

Hilditch says that one of the nicest things about being successful has been seeing her parents' pride in her achievements. 'When my father died I discovered that he had taped every television appearance of me talking about Crystal Clear. Whenever someone visited, he would say "Look at what Sharon has done."'

35

Rik Hellewell
Founder of Ovenu

A friend of Rik Hellewell's came back from a holiday in New Zealand and happened to mention that he had noticed an unusual barbecue-cleaning business out there that seemed to be doing well. Hellewell was intrigued. The operation was run by two men who would turn up in a van to dismantle the barbecue where it was. They would then clean it by immersing all the parts in an old cut-off oil drum filled with caustic soda.

His friend thought no more about it. But Hellewell did. He suddenly realised the concept might work in Britain – on domestic ovens. He says: 'At that time you could get someone to do your ironing and window cleaning and mow your lawn, but having your oven cleaned was one of the only things left indoors that you couldn't get done professionally. I realised that it was a niche market with big potential.'

Brought up in Bradford, West Yorkshire, Hellewell originally planned to become an engineer. He left school at 16 to take up an apprenticeship with a local engineering firm. But he soon realised it was not for him, and as soon as he had finished his apprenticeship he left to join a carpet and

upholstery cleaning company. He says: 'I was never very comfortable in a factory and being told what to do by people who didn't have the faintest idea themselves. I wanted to be the master of my own destiny.'

He stayed with the carpet-cleaning company for 10 years, rising to become a well-paid manager. But he always knew he wanted to run his own show one day, and had often thought the service sector offered the most potential. When his friend told him about the barbecue-cleaning business Hellewell knew it was the opportunity he had been waiting for. He quit his job, and using his knowledge of engineering spent £500 designing and building a portable cleaning tank that could hold every segment of a dismantled oven. Then he registered the design at the Patent Office to stop anyone stealing his idea.

Next he asked a local chemist to create a cleaning substance that, unlike existing products, did not contain caustic soda. That meant it could clean every part of the oven without damaging it. Hellewell says: 'We didn't want to turn up and do half a job. We wanted to be able to clean the whole appliance. And by registering the design of the equipment and by having our own products, we weren't going to make it easy for anyone else to come in and try to compete.'

Then he went to the local council tip and dragged home a couple of old ovens on which to test his new cleaning system. He admits: 'There was a lot of trial and error. There is only one way you can learn something brand new and that is to get stuck in and do it. I wanted to make all the mistakes myself first.'

When he was satisfied he had got it right, he had some leaflets printed and took out an advertisement in the local paper. Then he waited for the phone to ring. Luckily it did. In the first year Hellewell cleaned 368 ovens. It was hard work doing it all himself. But he deliberately chose to work alone, because from the start he decided that if the concept worked then he wanted to be able to use the data he had collected to turn his Ovenu business into a franchise operation.

Hellewell says that after working for a big company he was convinced franchising would be the best way to grow his business. 'When I was working in the carpet game we had 120 subcontractors and it was just wall-to-wall hassle,' he says. 'I wanted a system where people could own their business, but trade under a corporate identity. People who have got their own businesses tend to behave themselves

Fact file

Date of birth: 6 November 1958

Marital status: twice married with six children

Highest level of education achieved: grammar school

Qualifications: six O levels, OND in Engineering

Interests: rugby, golf, spending time with his children

Personal philosophy: 'Believe in yourself. If you have self-doubt you are not going to get there.'

better than subcontractors because they are responsible for the direction of their business. You don't get the Friday afternoon syndrome.'

In the end, however, it took Hellewell five years of running his business alone before he felt he had enough sales and marketing information to launch the franchise. He says: 'I was determined to make my business work. And if people know that the whole company is run by somebody who has been there, done it and got the T-shirt, they appreciate that and are going to want to work with you. There are a lot of companies being run by people who haven't got the faintest idea what goes on at the grass roots, and I don't think that is terribly bright.'

His single-mindedness has paid off. Hellewell now has 100 franchisees who pay a one-off fee of £7,250 to join Ovenu and a monthly fee of £145, producing a collective turnover of £3.5 million in 2004. Hellewell is now planning to expand his franchise overseas, first into continental Europe and then to North America and Australia.

Success has, however, come at a price. Hellewell thinks his focused determination to make the business work and his long working hours contributed to the breakdown of his first marriage. Now 46, he says: 'Anybody can be successful at whatever it is they want to do if they want to do it enough. But you have to be prepared to put in the extra hours and be blinkered. You are not born lucky, you make your own luck.'

But Hellewell says the sacrifices were worth it. He admits he is totally driven by the idea of being the best: 'If you are going to do something, you have to do it wholeheartedly with the ultimate objective of winning the race. Nobody ever remembers the person who came second. I tell my kids that it is not the taking part that counts, it is the winning. There is nothing that makes you feel as good as picking up the reward for your efforts.'

36

Jill Barker
Founder of Green Baby

Jill Barker opened her tiny Green Baby shop in Islington, north London, selling only one type of product – nappies. And most of them were washable nappies which hardly anyone used any more. She says: 'Everyone thought I was crazy. They thought it was just the silliest thing they had ever seen. They couldn't understand what I was doing selling washable nappies when there were all these fantastic disposable nappies out there. They didn't think anyone would come to my shop.'

Barker was brought up in Canada by her English mother and Dutch father, and after university spent five years backpacking around the world. She would often stop off in London for a few months at a time to earn some money by doing temping jobs in the City. So when she finally stopped travelling at the age of 25, she decided to stay in London, where she was offered a job at the banking group NatWest. After seven years she had risen to become a salesperson on the derivatives trading floor and was on a substantial salary.

At the age of 32, however, Barker had a baby and it changed her outlook on life. She returned to her job but

says: 'I realised I didn't want to be in the City any more. I was not enjoying it. I wanted to do something else.' She had also become increasingly interested in a very different subject. She says: 'My son got terrible rashes when I put nappies on him. So I started researching what goes into baby products – and it scared me.'

She tried to buy nappies that did not contain gels or chemicals, but when she discovered they were impossible to find in Britain, Barker decided the best solution would be to start up her own business selling natural baby products. So when she was made redundant from her City job soon afterwards, her payoff of £45,000 gave her all the motivation she needed to put her idea into practice.

Barker soon found, however, that not everyone thought it was a good plan. She says: 'I went to my local business centre for advice, but the adviser though it was a stupid idea and tried to convince me out of it. He said I shouldn't go into retailing because it was too difficult. I just ignored him and never went back to see him.'

Undaunted, she started sourcing chemical-free nappies from Sweden, Germany and Canada, and in 1999 opened a little shop, painting it bright pink so it would be noticed. Fortunately, her instincts were spot on. 'Everyone thought my shop was so bizarre that I had a lot of press coverage and so I had a huge following from day one,' she says. 'There were so many people out there, like me, who were searching for alternative products but could not find them. So when I opened my shop, it was like opening the floodgates.' She also discovered a surprisingly strong demand for washable nappies from parents who were concerned about the environmental impact of using disposable ones.

A few months after opening the shop, Barker decided to produce a mail-order catalogue as well. But she was reluctant to invest money in it without knowing how well it would do, so she and her staff would pack up the orders in the shop in the morning before customers arrived. When the mail-order side took off, however, Barker realised that the time had come for her to invest in a proper sales operation. In 2000 she invested £25,000 of her savings setting up a warehouse close to the shop. Her business now sells everything from toiletries to clothing, cots and bed sheets, and she has opened a second Green Baby shop in Notting Hill, west London.

Fact file

Date of birth: 12 March 1966

Marital status: married with one child

Highest level of education achieved: university

Qualifications: BA in Sociology from University of Calgary

Interests: skiing, horse-riding, hiking and camping

Personal philosophy: 'Work hard and take risks, and you will be rewarded.'

A few of her ideas did, however, prove unworkable. Barker originally hoped to be able to look after her baby at the same time as running the company, but she soon realised that this was not realistic. She says: 'I thought that because it was my business I could do what I wanted. But I quickly realised it was a really silly idea because I would spend all my time trying to sort out my baby. Or I would palm him off on the girls who worked in the shop and ask them to take him for a walk.'

Barker also realised quite early on she had to make a decision as to whether she wanted to run a small cottage industry, or to grow the business as much as she could. She chose the latter. She says: 'I could have stopped at that point and stayed as a nice cosy business and draw a nice salary from it. But I realised I couldn't stop – it wasn't in my nature. I wanted more. I decided I was onto a good thing and that it could grow. I thought I could make it a big business and create competition for the likes of Mothercare.'

Three years ago Barker persuaded her husband to join the business as a partner, and he now takes care of company finances. She plans to open another six shops over the next couple of years and the company is expected to have sales of £3 million for 2004. She says: 'I guess I'm a very ambitious person. I always have been.'

Now aged 38, Barker says the one disadvantage of running her own business is that she can never switch off. 'I miss the fact that when I was working in the City I could go home and shut off everything and I wouldn't have to think about what I would have to do tomorrow. But when you run your own business you are always thinking about what you have to do tomorrow.'

37

Matt Stevenson
Founder of Reef One

At the age of 10 Matt Stevenson had a goldfish called Jonny. But one day his sister decided to clean the stones in the goldfish bowl with bleach and sadly Jonny did not survive the experience. For Stevenson it was a pivotal moment. He says: 'I was upset but I was also confused because I could not understand why he had died when the tank had been cleaned. I didn't understand why you should not do certain things.'

He continued to keep fish as he grew up, gradually progressing from goldfish to tropical and marine fish. By the time he got to university he was carting round enormous fish tanks in the back of his car, and even rented a house so he could keep his fish with him. He decided to study product design, innovation and marketing at university, but soon discovered that his course had more in common with his fish-keeping than he had expected. 'Fish-keeping started off being just a hobby. But I realised that the skills I was learning in engineering and product design were lending themselves to solving some of the problems I had in keeping fish.'

In the end Stevenson decided to devote his third-year dissertation to designing and building an aquarium filter for specialist corals. It was at that point that he realised there might be a market for new fish-keeping products that were easier to maintain than those that were available at the time. So after graduating he spent a year studying the aquatics market and devising products for which he thought there might be a demand. He drew up a list of 12 ideas and after asking his family what they thought, decided to develop one further. It was a circular aquarium called the biOrb.

He says: 'This one product really stood out. It was basically a high-tech approach to the traditional fish bowl. The traditional fish bowl is cruel to fish because it doesn't have a filter and doesn't have a lot of water in it. This overcame all those problems.'

But not everyone was convinced that he was doing the right thing. He says: 'Most of my friends thought I was mad because they were all going off to earn decent amounts of money. I got a first-class degree, which meant I could have had a well-paid job straight away, but I didn't want to do that. I could see them thinking that perhaps Matt's got it wrong here. But I knew that what I had was good and that if I did it properly it could become a substantial business. So I could reap the rewards later on.'

Stevenson spent two months making a prototype in his parents' attic and in 1999 invited wholesalers and retailers round to take a look while his mum made them cups of tea. His belief in his product paid off. One wholesaler promptly put in an order for 1,000 biOrbs. On the strength of that single order, Stevenson decided to form a limited company, and bring his parents on board, one as a director, the other as company secretary.

He says: 'My father had just retired and he was obviously bored because he kept looking over my shoulder a lot saying, "That's interesting, what are you up to there?" Eventually it got to the point where he was sitting in on most of the meetings.'

Stevenson and his parents raised £30,000 between them to get the venture off the ground. His parents put in some of their savings while Stevenson raised his share by selling his sports car. Right from the start he decided to make the aquaria himself, and rented a small industrial unit to assemble parts that he sourced from around the world. 'I think

Fact file

Date of birth: 22 October 1975

Marital status: single

Highest level of education achieved: university

Qualifications: BSc (Hons) in Product Design, Innovation and Marketing from Derby University

Interests: scuba diving, motorsports

Personal philosophy: 'Lead, don't follow.'

part of the reason it has been so successful is because by making it ourselves we have learnt how to make it better and how to improve it,' he says.

The order for 1,000 units was quickly followed by a repeat order from the same wholesaler, and then another. In fact, the wholesaler was so determined to be the exclusive seller of the biOrb that for the first nine months he bought Stevenson's entire output. It was an enormous boost. Stevenson says: 'It allowed us to look at making the product properly rather than having to think about the selling side of it. We were selling them as fast as we could make them.'

His company Reef One now makes several versions of the biOrb. The company now has 15 full-time employees and sales in 2004 are expected to double to £4 million.

Stevenson says his mission is to take away some of the confusion that surrounds fish-keeping. 'When people go into a fish shop they are faced with a bewildering list of things to buy, but most people don't want to know how to wire up a fish tank or what chemicals to add. They just want to keep fish. So our job is to work that all out for them and take away those question marks.'

Now 29, he puts his success down to a combination of determination and self-confidence: 'It took a lot of self-belief because a lot of people didn't understand what we were trying to achieve. It was dogged determination, long hours and hard work.'

He still keeps about 30 fish as a hobby, and last year bought himself a brand new sports car to replace the one he had been forced to sell. 'It was at that point I realised I had come full circle,' he says. 'I always dreamt about doing a James Dyson and it is very exciting to be achieving it. It is the stuff of schoolboy dreams.'

38

Sally Wilton
Founder of etc Venues

When Sally Wilton started her own company providing training and conference facilities, she was determined to present a highly professional image so that clients would think they were dealing with a much larger company. The illusion was, however, short-lived. Just a few weeks after opening, her nanny called in sick at the last minute so Wilton had to take her baby in to work. Then the tea lady failed to show up as well. So Wilton ended up having to push the tea trolley round to clients herself – with her six-month old son asleep on the bottom shelf. She says: 'The first few weeks were really chaotic. We had to learn very quickly about everything. We just survived on adrenalin and enthusiasm.'

Fortunately, Wilton already had a lot of experience dealing with challenging situations. Brought up in Nigeria, where her father worked for the government, her life was turned upside down at the age of eight when she was sent to boarding school in Northern Ireland. Within a year she had been expelled for disruptive behaviour. She says: 'I had an absolutely idyllic childhood out in Nigeria, and I was a very happy child. But when I came to Ireland I went to boarding

school and it was a very unhappy experience. I just found the rules and regulations very difficult to understand. I never did grasp the concept of walking in a crocodile.'

Wilton dreamt of escaping Ireland to become a zoologist, and when she left university she got a job on a fish farm in Canada before heading to Tanzania to manage a trout farm. 'I could see Mount Kilimanjaro from my veranda,' she says. 'It was the most physically beautiful place I have ever been to. It was terrifically exciting.'

But at the age of 26, Wilton realised she had other priorities in her life. She explains: 'Fish farming was very interesting, but it was also quite lonely because I was by myself and I realised the chances of meeting and having a relationship with somebody would be quite low. I decided it was time to move on.' She returned to London but found it impossible to get work. She ended up spending a year doing odd jobs painting and decorating.

She says: 'I applied for about 100 jobs doing anything and everything but I didn't get a single interview. It taught me a lot about being unemployed and not being able to afford the bus fare to go somewhere.' Eventually Wilton found a job providing business advice to worker co-operatives, and then moved to work for a venture capital company.

However, she soon realised that the firm was being held back by the high cost of renting the space it used. She decided there might be a gap in the market for a business that provided affordable training and conference venues which companies could hire from half a day to several months. As well as the space itself, she could provide clients with everything from data projectors and sound systems to lunch and evening drinks receptions.

The only problem was finding a suitable place to hire out. But that dilemma was solved when the man who owned a nearby building offered her 4,000 square feet of empty space at a low rent to get started. Wilton quit her job, persuading three colleagues from her old firm to join her, and invested her life savings of £15,000 in the venture, spending the money on setting up a kitchen in the building and buying art for the walls.

'I felt very strongly that the company should try to present an image of how we wanted to be, rather than how we were,' she says. 'In reality, we had to do everything

Fact file

Date of birth: 27 June 1955

Marital status: separated with two children

Highest level of education achieved: university

Qualifications: BSc in Zoology from Durham University, MSc in Aquaculture and Fisheries Management from Stirling University

Interests: cinema, art, reading, walking and managing stroppy teenagers

Personal philosophy: 'Failure is not an option. Success is a result of hard work and a bit of luck.'

ourselves from moving the furniture at night to doing the waitressing.'

The concept took off, and as demand for her services grew she took over more and more space until she eventually bought the whole building. But then came September 11. Orders dried up and competition intensified as hotels scrabbled for conference business to compensate for the downturn in the number of American visitors.

Wilton says: 'From being in a position where it seemed like we could do nothing wrong, suddenly we were faced with a price war as hotels became fierce competitors. We had to reassess the whole business. I worked as hard as I had when I started it up.'

In a strange way, however, the setback also proved rewarding. She says: 'If the truth be told I had become a bit bored because the business wasn't as challenging as it had been. But when this happened it became much more intellectually stimulating and fun again. From having been a reactive company where we were just taking people's business, we suddenly had to be much more proactive and work very closely with our clients again. It re-energised me and business became a thrilling adventure again.'

In an effort to get back on track, Wilton employed a business development manager and invested heavily to secure sales. It worked. The company will have sales of £8.4 million for 2004. It now has five venues across London and employs 130 people.

Wilton, now aged 47 says: 'I have been really lucky because everything I have done I have really enjoyed. My father was a big influence on me because he had a number of careers and enjoyed each one in very different ways, and that has guided me through all of this.' She adds: 'I think if you don't wake up in the morning and think, "I really want to do this, I really love it," then you shouldn't be doing it.'

39

Charlie Bigham
Founder of Bighams

Charlie Bigham had a comfortable life in London and a well-paid job with a management consultancy, but he had always wanted to start his own business. So when he was 28 he gave up his job, bought a camper van and spent nine months driving overland to India with his girlfriend in the hope of finding inspiration.

He found it while eating food in local markets along the way. He says: 'I suddenly realised my business should be about food and preparing the ingredients to be cooked quickly, because that is what everybody does around the world. If you go into a market in Turkey or Morocco, there will be somebody with a stall and a bunch of fresh ingredients – you sit down in front of them and they just toss them in a pan, and it's ready. I realised that convenience doesn't have to mean putting something in a microwave and pressing a button. It can mean quick, fresh food.'

Bigham initially toyed with the idea of opening a chain of shops in the UK selling fresh ingredients. But he soon decided the best plan would be to set up a business preparing fresh food kits for people to cook themselves at home.

Brought up in London and Ireland, Bigham studied English literature at university but had always had an interest in food. 'To me, the best meal is when you come home starving and there's nothing in the fridge, but then you find something hidden in a corner and something else in the store cupboard and you're forced to think creatively about what you are going to eat,' he says. 'You can have some really legendary meals.'

By the time he got back to London in 1996, Bigham was ready to put his plan into action. He sold the camper van to buy a computer, and got a job in a delicatessen in order to gain experience of working with food. He also started experimenting in his kitchen, preparing dishes of Cajun chicken, salmon and zesty Caribbean lamb. Then he called up Waitrose, the supermarket chain, to see if it would be interested in stocking his food kits. It said yes. He says: 'I just rang the switchboard and said I had this great idea. I got put through to somebody who said, "Come in and show it to us."'

There were, however, a few hurdles to clear before the business could be set up. Bigham had to contact 15 banks before he found one prepared to let him open a business account, even though he was not asking to borrow anything and was investing £20,000 of his own money in the venture. He also had to change his product. He started out producing complete meal kits, but after doing cooking demonstrations in stores and talking to customers he quickly realised they wanted something different.

He says: 'They were saying they loved the salmon and watercress sauce, but they didn't like the fact that we had put broccoli with it – or they didn't want to pay a premium for potatoes or rice because they already had some at home. So we switched from making meal kits to doing marinaded meat or fish plus a sauce, because those are the bits that most people don't want to do themselves.'

After three years Bigham hit another hurdle. He had rented a small catering unit to prepare his products, but one day Waitrose told him that the premises did not meet its stringent health and safety standards. If he wanted to continue to supply their supermarkets, he would have to move to larger premises. Bigham told them he would be happy to do so – provided Waitrose gave him more business so he could finance the move.

Fact file

Date of birth: 21 April 1967

Marital status: married with four children

Highest level of education achieved: university

Qualifications: MA (Hons) in English Literature from Edinburgh University

Interests: travel, being outside, preferably near the sun or up a mountain; going to the theatre

Personal philosophy: 'Enjoy what you do and take pride in it because then you will do it well.'

His quick thinking paid off. The following week Waitrose tripled its order, and Bigham suddenly went from supplying four recipes to 50 shops to supplying 12 recipes to 70 shops. He says: 'I came to work one day and the company was three times as big as it had been the day before.'

Bigham decided to move the business into premises five times bigger, at a cost of more than £1 million. He footed the bill with the help of a £70,000 grant from the Department of Trade and Industry, a £30,000 grant from a local enterprise agency and a £250,000 bank loan secured through the Small Firms Loan Guarantee scheme. Happily, the investment paid off. Bigham's now produces 70 different dishes, is expected to achieve sales of £7.5 million in 2004, and is about to move into even bigger premises.

Now 37 and married with four children, Bigham says he is driven by the desire to enjoy what he does – and to be free to decide exactly how he spends his life. He says: 'I'm not very good at working for other people. I don't like being told what to do. I like being in control of my own destiny. It's very simple – I'm trying to have a good time. We spend many hours at work, and I find it hugely depressing that a lot of people go to work and hate it. I feel hugely privileged that I come to work and enjoy it.'

Bigham says his only regret was not having the courage to start his own business sooner. 'I was dilly-dallying, thinking shall I, shan't I? But I should have just started it because even when I was working 22 hours a day and being paid nothing it was still more fun than working for someone else. These days when people ask my advice about starting up a business, I tell them, "Just do it now."'

40

Philip Hughes
Founder of The Ice Box

At one time the words 'ice sculpture' meant carved swans and dolphins at seafood buffets on cruise ships. Not any more. These days an ice sculpture might easily be anything from a chandelier to a work of art or a life-size model of a car. It may even have freezing-cold vodka flowing through the middle of it. Much of this transformation is due to the efforts of Philip Hughes, whose company, The Ice Box, has spent the past 11 years reinventing the concept of ice sculptures by dreaming up stunning creations for film premieres and showbiz parties. For the opening of the Baltic Mills gallery in Newcastle his team spent weeks creating a full-size model of an Audi TT. For the royal premiere of the Bond film *Die Another Day* it built a 30-metre drinks bar entirely from ice.

Born in Lancashire, Hughes's childhood was divided between boarding school in Sussex and Africa and the West Indies, where his father worked for a big oil company. He would often stay in lovely hotels, and decided he wanted to work in one when he was older. So when he left school at

the age of 18 he joined a management training scheme with Holiday Inn and gradually worked his way up the industry.

Hughes was on holiday with his family in Boston, Massachusetts, when he visited an ice-making factory and suddenly realised that ice could have huge commercial potential in Britain too. He says: 'I had always been fascinated by ice sculptures, but in Britain they were so cheesy. Then I realised it didn't just have to be a lump of ice carved in the shape of a swan. You could do so much more with it. In America they are in another league when it comes to ice sculpture. People don't think twice about getting one to celebrate any kind of family occasion. Yet nobody in Britain had spotted the potential market opportunities. I thought it would be a wonderful thing to do.'

Hughes also thought there might be a demand for a round-the-clock ice-delivery business which delivered according to the demands of the customer rather than the supplier. He says: 'If a bartender runs out of ice at 5 o'clock in the evening, he needs more right then, not at 7 o'clock the following morning. But suppliers would say they would be there and wouldn't show up, and when they eventually did, the ice would have turned into bags of water.'

Turning his vision into reality was, however, a bold step. By this time Hughes had a well-paid job as operations director with Forte, the hotel group, and he and his wife had just had their first baby. He says: 'I had a comfortable corporate existence and I would go on research trips to America and France, staying in the best hotels. My friends thought I was mad to leave. But I wanted to get the entrepreneurial juices flowing and create something of my own.'

He took a course in ice-sculpting, then he spent the family's entire life savings of £15,000 together with a £5,000 grant from Wandsworth Enterprise Agency buying an ice-making machine and a van. He says: 'At the beginning my wife and I used to sit in a cafe with a mobile phone just waiting for it to ring with an order. There were times when I said, "What am I doing? I could have had a company car and weekends off."'

To his relief, however, he discovered there was more than enough demand for his cubes and sculptures to make his vision work. He says: 'In the first year we completely surprised ourselves because the business did better than

Fact file

Date of birth: 11 August 1959

Marital status: married with three children

Highest level of education achieved: college

Qualifications: HND in Hospitality Management from Westminster College

Interests: fine wines, food, classic cars

Personal philosophy: 'To succeed at anything in life you have to apply passion.'

we thought it would. We hadn't anticipated earning any-thing out of it in our plan and yet it made a return. It was a bit of a boost. And then in the second year that more than doubled.'

As the business grew Hughes initially found it hard to deal with the changing nature of his relationship with his employees. He says: 'I had to go through an evolution process as we outgrew being a cottage industry. As the business grew I was not at the coalface as much and so was not there to motivate people on a daily basis. So I had to intro-duce systems to maintain the quality and standards. That was very tough.'

Eleven years on, however, his gamble has paid off. The Ice Box now has its own automated ice-making factory and is the biggest supplier of ice cubes in London. It employs 25 people and in 2004 is expected to have sales of around £3 million. It was asked to create a replica of the Euro 2004 Cup in ice for the football tournament in Portugal, and in recog-nition of the role he plays in the industry Hughes was recently appointed president of the International Special Events Society.

Hughes, now 45, says that becoming an entrepreneur has changed him in unexpected ways: 'In a funny way it has made me less obsessed with success for success's sake. And it has made me less greedy. Although I am earning more, on a personal level I am even better off. It has made me a better communicator and more thoughtful about other people because every day I am dealing with a real cross-section of them.'

He has no regrets about taking the plunge. 'I live or die by my own success now. The buzz is incomparable. I think life is about using the passion and energy you have, and every day I am doing what I want to do and that is a great feeling. I really believe that if you want to do something enough, then you should do it. Because if you don't, you will regret it.'